"Ménard is a leader in the field. His book teaches the importance of mental training and how it can help you step up your game when the heat is on."
PAT BRISSON — NHLPA agent — Co-Head of CAA Hockey

"The mental training techniques used by JF in elite sport and the performing arts are equally transferable to many fields of human performance."
BERNARD PETIOT — vice-president — casting and performance — Cirque du Soleil

"Thanks to the mental training techniques shared in this book, we overcame our fears and gave it our best on the ice. There's no greater gift for an athlete!"
SCOTT MOIR and TESSA VIRTUE — figure skaters — three-time Olympic champions

"This book provides managers with the tools to adopt a winning attitude and better coach their teams to reach a higher level."
PATRICK CHARBONNEAU — vice president — PepsiCo Beverages Canada

"I always knew how to manage the pressure, but, with JF Menard's advice, I was able to take things to the next level. He really helped me to avoid distractions and focus on the right things. When I'm in the starting gate, there's no doubt in my mind! A big part of my success on the slopes comes from excellent mental performance coaching."
MIKAËL KINGSBURY — freestyle skier — Olympic champion and four-time world champion

"This is the ideal book for our times. Resiliency is the key asset as we navigate these uncharter rançois' tips, tricks, and techniq owth is

guaranteed. The real success of this book is how these practices are achievable for *everyone*. Not just the superstar athletes."
JEANNE-MARIE ROBILLARD — National Speakers Bureau

"JF's principles help me cope with stressful moments. Now, I am capable of managing my emotions when needed and I know how to become confident when it counts the most. Finding solutions to my challenges has become easier than ever! The teachings in this book are undoubtedly important contributors to my success."
MAX PARROT — professional snowboarder — Olympic medalist, eight-time X Games gold medalist, cancer survivor

"Thanks to this book, you'll understand how you can train your brain the way great athletes do to improve your performance."
ROBERTO MARROCCO — vice-president, portfolio manager and member of Chairman's Council — RBC Dominion Securities

"The strength of this book lies in an approach based on experience, research, and observation, but mostly on the authors' deep desire to motivate individuals to excel and achieve their goals."
NICOLAS GILL — two-time Olympic medalist — CEO and High-Performance Director — Judo Canada

"Thanks to an authentic and user-friendly approach, you'll learn easy-to-use strategies to build your confidence, rebound after failure, and persevere when under pressure."
DOMINICK GAUTHIER — co-founder of B2ten Foundation, former Olympian and coach of Olympic medal-winning athletes

Train (Your Brain) Like an Olympian

Train (Your Brain) Like an Olympian

Gold Medal Techniques to Unleash
Your Potential at Work

Jean François Ménard

with Marie Malchelosse

Translated by Linda Hilpold

Published by ECW Press
665 Gerrard Street East
Toronto, Ontario, Canada M4M 1Y2
416-694-3348 / info@ecwpress.com

Cover design: Sonya Clarry
Translator: Linda Hilpold
Author photo: © Julia Marois

LIBRARY AND ARCHIVES CANADA CATALOGUING IN
PUBLICATION

Title: Train (your brain) like an olympian : gold medal
techniques to unleash your potential at work /
Jean François Ménard, with Marie Malchelosse ;
translated by Linda Hilpold.

Other titles: L'olympien au bureau. English

Names: Ménard, Jean François, 1982– author. |
Malchelosse, Marie, author.

Description: Translation of: L'olympien au bureau :
la préparation mentale des grands athlètes transposée
au monde du travail.

Identifiers: Canadiana (print) 20200266683
Canadiana (ebook) 20200266764

ISBN 978-1-77041-590-4 (softcover)
ISBN 978-1-77305-438-4 (PDF)
ISBN 978-1-77305-437-7 (EPUB)

Subjects: LCSH: Psychology, Industrial. | LCSH:
Attitude (Psychology) | LCSH: Achievement
motivation. | LCSH: Athletes—Psychology.

Classification: LCC HF5548.8 .M4613 2021
DDC 158.7—dc23

The publication of *Train (Your Brain) Like an Olympian* has been funded in part by the Government of Canada. *Ce livre est
financé en partie par le gouvernement du Canada*. We acknowledge the contribution of the Government of Ontario through
Ontario Creates for the marketing of this book.

PRINTED AND BOUND IN CANADA

PRINTING: MARQUIS   5   4

CONTENTS

ACKNOWLEDGMENTS

Jean François

I would like to begin by thanking Marie. Your writing is one of a kind. Writing down my ideas wasn't an easy task, yet you did just that, and better than I could ever have imagined. Our teamwork was gold medal worthy!

Thank you to the publisher, ECW, who believed in the project from the start.

Thank you to B2ten for allowing me to help Canadian athletes achieve their dreams.

Thank you as well to the athletes, artists, and others, whose stories I've included in this book. I will always be grateful to you for agreeing to be a part of it. Without you, this book wouldn't be the same.

Thank you to all my clients. Because of you I get to do the greatest job in the world.

Lastly, thank you to my family for your support and patience. I love you, Manon, Niko, and Kieva.·

Marie

I would like to thank Jean François. I had the pleasure to explore your thoughts and collect your wisdom for many months. Your desire to help others shines through all the theories, tips, and strategies. I hope that I was able to find the right words to demonstrate your passion for your work.

Many thanks to the amazing team at ECW.

Thank you to my dear friend, Isabelle Lafortune. You may not have known this, but your kind presence showed me the way.

Lastly, thank you, Gabriel, my son and number one supporter. How is it possible to be the mom of such an amazing person? It's an unbelievable privilege. You knew long before I did that I had what it would take to see this project through. Thank you for being as proud of me as I am of you, and so much more.

FOREWORD

At the beginning of my professional football career, I thought that I would continually improve my physical strength over the years. Given the countless number of hours spent on the football field and in the gym, I expected that improvement on the physical testing results that I obtained during the NFL Scouting Combine would happen naturally.

Despite my sustained efforts on the field and in the gym, the reality is that I would struggle to get the same results I got seven years ago. It was wishful thinking to believe that my body was going to get significantly stronger and faster. The physical demands of a contact sport like football make it nearly impossible to stay in tip-top shape for an entire season. A charley horse prevents you from doing squats one week, while a bruised shoulder prevents you from bench-pressing the next. Realistically, it's only during the off-season that you can rebuild strength and explosiveness.

Still, most players find ways to polish their technique. During the season, we perfect different skills during practice. In my case, as an offensive lineman, blocking is my forte. Yet I've realized throughout my career that the most decisive factor in becoming a better football player is the mental game.

During a game, I go through sixty to eighty plays. In theory, there's no link between one play and the next. The most important thing I have learned is to turn the page after each play so that I can focus on the next one. In essence, I mentally reset sixty times during a game. Resetting is easy when things are going well, but doing it when you just made a bad play in the fourth quarter and eighty thousand people are staring at you is not so easy!

Developing robust grittiness, self-confidence, and focusing abilities are what really challenges an athlete. These psychological factors differentiate an average player from a great player. Athletes spend so much time training to become physically fit; there's no reason not to do the same with mental skills.

Over the last seven years, I've balanced being a professional football player with being a medical student at McGill University. Through several clinical clerkships, I noticed that the mental skills used on a football field are just as useful in a hospital environment. Whether it's reviewing a differential diagnosis during a critical situation, correctly answering the questions asked by my medical supervisor, or writing a nerve-wracking final exam, having a trained mind allows you to perform in a logical and rational way.

From my first meeting with Jean François, I noticed right away that his extensive experience and notable expertise make him an undeniable leader in his field. Thanks to our discussions, I realized that training the mind is a key component in reaching my full potential. To become a winner on the football field, in the emergency room, or at the office, the same skills are needed to perform: having the right attitude, knowing how to eliminate distractions, demonstrating leadership, and overcoming your fears. His guidance has undoubtedly helped me play at my best and help my team win the Super Bowl.

LAURENT DUVERNAY-TARDIF
GUARD FOR THE KANSAS CITY CHIEFS
OF THE NATIONAL FOOTBALL LEAGUE,
SUPER BOWL LIV CHAMPIONS

INTRODUCTION

A High Performer in the Making

Have no fear, dear reader! This isn't about racing up the twenty-two floors of your office building or doing five sets of a hundred push-ups at your workstation. Being an Olympian[1] at work is less painful but can be just as gratifying as being an Olympic athlete performing in front of a global audience.

The goal here is to transfer the mental training strategies that allow an Olympian to perform at any given time — whatever the circumstances — to your working life.

"Performance" is a concept that is often misunderstood and usually associated with a performer who is exceptional in their field. The goal of *Train (Your Brain) Like an Olympian* is not to make you the best in the world in your field, but to offer you ways to improve, period.

But why is it important to learn how to perform better?

Well, in the whirlwind of everyday life, we rarely stop to think about it, yet, for better or worse, we're called upon to excel, just like an Olympian.

---

1   Although the term "Olympian" normally refers to the gods of Greek mythology living in Olympia, we've decided to use it in this book to only describe high-level athletes who compete in the Olympic Games.

We all have to perform, whether we're nurses, clerks, teachers, police officers, project managers, or parents, and we all have people who expect something from us, including bosses, customers, shareholders, bankers, colleagues, and children. The same principle applies to high-level athletes, who have to meet the expectations of their coach, their federation, their sponsors, and, ultimately, their country. So, without realizing it, you, too, need to perform, just like an Olympian.

We said it right from the start: it's not about training your body like an Olympian, although a growing number of professionals find physical exercise, such as running or cycling, to be an effective antidote to stress. Instead, the book will focus on an aspect that both elite athletes and office workers need to perform optimally: mental training.

You've often heard it said that athletic performance isn't just physical but also mental. That's where *Train (Your Brain) Like an Olympian* comes into play.

Your brain is your main tool, your engine, your secret weapon. In the sports world, there's a point at which the best athletes have reached similar physical and technical skill sets, and it becomes more about what's under the helmet that sets the champions apart. They've trained their brains to focus better, to react well to unexpected changes, to deal with pressure, and ultimately to perform better.

But wait! The brain can play tricks on us. It is an engine that must be well maintained. There are Olympians who, in spite of their training, fail to send the right message to their brains, and they choke or collapse when they should excel. Their brains have become their worst enemy.

The Olympians who triumph at the Games owe it to a brain that's as highly trained as their body. They never let their brains steal *their* moment. Likewise, a worker doesn't want to be robbed of *their* moment by their brain.

Is your boss a former athlete?

The March 2004 issue of *Fortune* revealed that 90 percent of the CEOs of that year's Fortune 500 companies are former high-level athletes. Surprised? You shouldn't be. All skills being equal, employers will often choose a former athlete over another candidate. Employers are won over by athletes' resiliency, their ability to work in a team, their receptiveness to learning, and their ability to perform under pressure. Athletes are go-getters. They'll do whatever it takes to reach their goals. Any employer can only dream of a profile like this, right?

There are many parallels to be drawn between the world of sports and the workplace.

- The athlete prepares for the next game; the director of sales prepares for the next meeting.
- The athlete deals with the stress of performing in front of twenty thousand spectators and runs the risk of disappointing them if they fail; the president deals with the stress of making a decision that could cost the company five million dollars if they make a mistake.
- The athlete controls their breathing before a free throw that could win the game; the account manager controls their breathing before meeting the person who could become the company's biggest customer.
- The skier adapts to the changing snow conditions; the worker adapts to technological change.
- The athlete endures physical pain; the worker endures the fatigue of a twelve-hour day.

You get the idea.

As a result, a worker needs mental toughness just as much as an athlete does, and in some cases, maybe more. Surprised again? Let's dig a little deeper.

Most athletes lead a fairly simple life that is managed like clockwork by a whole host of professionals. A lot of things are decided for them — training schedules, nutrition plans, treatment sessions, psychological support, sleeping strategies, and competition preparation. Most have no children and few responsibilities outside of their sport, which makes it easier to focus entirely on their craft.

It's not that simple for workers.

At the office, we're expected to always be busy, managing loads of emails, adapting to new technological gadgets, or constantly flipping back and forth between different files. You're focusing on one task when, out of the blue, someone barges into your office and asks you to urgently work on another. At the end of it all, you realize that it wasn't really that urgent, rather more like a waste of time and energy. The demands pile up. At the end of the day, you heave a big sigh. Whew! Your day is done . . . or is it?

After work, there's still the family and household to take care of, assisting your children with their homework, paying bills, maintaining your relationship with your spouse, performing domestic chores, and a whole host of other responsibilities.

Athletes know what to expect. Their schedule is detailed in a document called the yearly training program, which lays out exactly what they have to do, week in and week out, for the entire year: the number of gym sessions, specific training volumes, intensity loads, logical lead-ups for competition, even when to rest and recover. The athletes know well in advance when they'll have to face moments of high pressure and stress, thereby enabling them to prepare accordingly. The future is predictable.

In contrast, Olympians at work are regularly put to the test. Several times during the week, they'll be called on to respond to challenges, meet deadlines, play different roles, take care of unexpected issues, and manage ever-changing schedules. They experience many moments of stress on a daily basis. They're also occasionally exposed to moments of significant stress that can't always be anticipated and for which they're often unprepared.

It is now common practice for athletes to have access to a *mental performance coach*. This specialized coach teaches an athlete how to train their brain to perform well in a situation involving constant distractions.

How many of you can count on a mental performance coach to help manage daily challenges at work?

Bingo!

That's why, in today's turbulent world, workers have to take it upon themselves to find out what psychological tools are needed to improve and excel. Remember that your brain is your engine. In other words, the outcome of your work is directly linked to your ability to perform mentally.

As we like to say, it's better to invest in your brain than in your work!

When it comes to work, it's never enough!

In the workplace, employees commonly receive specialized technical training, which helps improve their job performance. However, not as much is offered in regard to human performance skills: how to be more efficient, how to deal with failure, how to manage stress, how to organize time better, and how to maximize energy. Athletes are taught these performance skills and practice them regularly, but not workers.

Does this make sense?

Employees are asked to maintain a frenetic pace and "do more with less," an impossible ask that has more to do with wishful thinking than efficiency. A worker is forced to respond, but how?

The demands multiply and the expectations increase on a daily basis, not to mention the pressure to become a technologically savvy world-champion multitasker. Think about it: How many of you only do what is written in your job description? Yep, you're not alone!

Here's a situation that frequently occurs: An employee has just had a successful year, yet her boss not only congratulated her but asked her *how she could do more* in the coming year, leaving her completely at a loss. This is our new reality: someone always wants more. The business world is competitive and always focused on more, more, more. As we rush from one demand to the next, it's easy to run out of breath.

The U.S. Army created an acronym to help soldiers prepare strategically for complicated missions: VUCA, four letters that stand for volatile, uncertain, complex, and ambiguous. Let's admit it: these words accurately describe many workplaces and define today's working world quite well. Essentially, you need to have a strong head on your shoulders to calmly navigate these choppy waters.

> Being mentally tough in the workplace twenty years ago was considered an additional asset to the job. Today, mental toughness is a necessity.

The working environment (e.g., demands, expectations, requirements) may have changed a lot, but our brains have not. In the last twenty years, the way in which the brain operates hasn't changed at all! The neurological connections and brain waves are the same. Mental skills, however, are not static; they evolve over time, hence the importance of developing them to become better performers at work.

Twenty years ago, there were no smartphones glued to our hands. For most people, the nine-to-five workday was normal, and the work stayed at work. Now, our electronic devices follow us home. The temptation to extend the workday into the evening is strong, isn't it? A message left in a voice mail at noon on Friday could be answered on Monday, even Tuesday. But today, we do just about everything in a hurry.

Tempted to turn back the clock?

Increasingly, companies are coming to realize that employees are exhausted from working in this new reality. Managers are starting to recognize the relevance of providing employees with the psychological tools they need and allocating additional financial resources for talks and workshops on various topics related to mental training. The change has started, even if there is still a long way to go.

You may not have access to this kind of training in your workplace or a mental performance coach to guide you like Olympians have. However, nothing is stopping you from getting the tools that will allow you to discover the Olympian within you and we are here to help, bringing our expertise to this text.

Writing this book: a team effort

As you read this book, you'll get to learn more about the fascinating world of elite sports. As professionals, we've been privileged to witness many talented performers achieve some remarkable feats; the performance world has been in our lives for quite some time. Allow us to introduce ourselves . . .

Jean François Ménard

As far back as I can remember, I have felt a profound need to help people achieve their wildest dreams. This has led to the work I do today: advising the elite athletes who come to my office for help. Sometimes I also coach them during competitions around the world.

My job is so rewarding. Helping an athlete to identify a mental obstacle that is holding them back and finding ways to overcome it generates an indescribable feeling of gratification. Each of these moments becomes my very own *Olympic medal*.

Fresh out of graduate school, I ran away with the circus, joining the world-famous entertainment company Cirque du Soleil. It opened the door to a fascinating world of artists:

acrobats, musicians, clowns, fire-spitters, jugglers — I could go on and on. They were the *crème de la crème* from around the world, representing forty different nationalities. As a first job, it was certainly hard to beat!

The Cirque du Soleil artists have a demanding job, performing hundreds of times a year with few breaks. I quickly noticed that proper mental training was key to succeeding onstage. I dove into the experience headfirst! Circus life is challenging yet fascinating. Once you've worked in a circus, you can work anywhere!

Five years later, I left the big top for the Olympic arena. At the end of my graduate studies, I remember saying to a group of professors that someday I would be working with one of the world's best athletes. I didn't know it at the time but my prediction would come true in less than ten years, and there would be more than *one* athlete. I experienced some extraordinary moments with some of the greatest Canadian Olympians, including Scott Moir and Tessa Virtue in figure skating, Mikaël Kingsbury in freestyle skiing, Maxence Parrot in snowboarding, Derek Drouin and Damian Warner in track and field, and Antoine Valois-Fortier in judo. My work with these athletes during the 2016 Olympic Games in Rio and the 2018 Games in PyeongChang translated into several Olympic medals. The Olympic adventure continues: at the time of writing, I'm coaching about a dozen athletes for the 2020 and 2022 Olympic Games. As the saying goes, be careful what you wish for!

Please note that all of the Olympians mentioned in this book generously agreed to my sharing with you some moments that we experienced together. Their stories will help you better understand how they used mental training principles to prepare for major events and, ultimately, achieve their goals. I would like to thank them for their participation.

Obviously, the success that these high-level athletes achieved is the result of the work of a group of experts working together. In fact, to reach the top, an athlete is surrounded by a team of specialists: strength and conditioning coaches, technical coaches,

physiologists, medical practitioners, nutritionists, sports therapists, and agents. Mental performance coaching is just one piece
of the puzzle in this team effort.

As a public speaker, my focus is to teach the mental training
concept first, then communicate the strategies associated with the
concept that the participants will be able to use in their workplace.
I'm an educator, not a motivator. If people walk away at the end of
my talks motivated and inspired, so much the better; however, my
main objective remains to ensure that they leave better equipped.
I decided to use the same method for this book.

After attending a talk, participants often say to me, "You
should write a book." Well, here it is, along with everything else
that I don't have time to explain during a one-hour talk!

This book is for you, the Olympian at work.

Marie Malchelosse

I first met Jean François (JF) for an interview during which he told
me his fascinating experience at the PyeongChang Olympic Games.
I, too, was in South Korea, reporting on the Games. I was standing
at the bottom of the moguls course and witnessed Canadian freestyle skiing superstar Mikaël Kingsbury's spectacular win.

During this interview a few weeks after the Games, JF detailed
what had happened that evening. He spoke about Mikaël's state
of mind, as well as what the coaches experienced. He explained
how each word spoken to Mikaël mattered. How the tone of their
voices could send the wrong signal to him. How everyone had to
be in tune and believe in all the work that they had done together
during the last four years in anticipation of this very moment. In
fact, JF told the story from a unique vantage point, which no one
else had, including me.

In more than twenty years as a journalist, I have followed dozens
of athletes. I had experienced the Olympic Games, witnessed
triumphs and failures. I've always known that the mental game can
play a decisive role in the final outcome, and I've written articles on

it. This issue has been talked about for a long time. Yet, during JF's account, I saw mental performance coaching from a new angle. I noted its scale and scope. In the end, everything has to be taken into account to allow no doubt to enter the athlete's mind.

It immediately became clear that more people had to hear about mental performance coaching — not just athletes. From the moment of that interview on, the decision to join forces with JF to write this book was a no-brainer.

How to use this book

Train (Your Brain) Like an Olympian doesn't claim to revolutionize your life. On the contrary. You know your own situation best, and you must decide what will work for you or not.

Really, its sole claim is to offer the same tools that Olympians use to achieve excellence and reach their goals. These tools can be applied to a multitude of situations in our professional lives, including:

- how to deal with stress
- how to face difficult moments with a constructive mindset
- how to remain confident even when feeling vulnerable
- how to be comfortable with the uncomfortable

These tools will be explained and illustrated using real-life stories experienced with JF's clients, and for that reason, we chose to use the singular pronoun "I" throughout the book as if he alone were speaking to you. You'll have special access to the world of Olympians and other elite performers. You'll bear witness to their drive to perform, and you'll learn how they incorporated the mental performance tools during their quest for success. We'll also share with you some of JF's personal experiences — his aspirations, his preparation for the Olympic Games, important lessons that have helped him grow, and so on.

We easily learn by observation, so we included some illustrations to explain some of the drier concepts to make them easier to understand. You'll notice that the drawings are hand-drawn just as they are on the white board in JF's office.

Take ownership of this book. If some of the chapters are totally relevant and get you thinking, so much the better. Other sections of the book may be less so, and that's as it should be. There's no quick fix. Take notes. Doodle. Stop and reflect. Anything goes.

On your mark. Get set. Go!

CHAPTER 1

Seize Every Opportunity to Learn

All the athletes I know have one thing in common: they have a strong desire to excel. They are constantly looking to become stronger, tougher, and faster. Their daily motivation is to simply get better.

Figure skaters Scott Moir and Tessa Virtue exemplify this constant striving to improve. During their illustrious career, Scott and Tessa won the most Olympic medals in the history of figure skating while also becoming the first North Americans to win Olympic gold in ice dance. Their success had nothing to do with luck. They used strict training methods with military-like discipline. Ultimately, their approach was plain and simple: every day they would ask themselves, "How can we be better?"

During our mental training sessions, Scott and Tessa took reams and reams of notes — Tessa alone filled two large notebooks! Between appointments, they constantly reread their notes from the previous week so they could apply the mental training strategies during practices. Before they showed up for sessions, I had to make sure I was ready, because as soon as they sat down in my office they began peppering me with questions:

- How can I stay focused when my legs feel dead?
- What can we do to trigger a burst of self-confidence just before stepping out on the ice?
- How can I remain calm and regain control when my inner chatter is negative and pessimistic?
- What can we do to improve communication with our coaches?

They challenged me and everyone else on their team: their skating coaches, their nutritionist, their strength and conditioning trainers, and their therapists. Every small lesson learned was taken seriously. They brought their notebooks everywhere to ensure that they didn't forget anything. They would go over their notes regularly, whether on a plane, over coffee, or at the rink during warm-ups.

They were surrounded by a dozen experts in a variety of disciplines to help them prepare for the 2018 Games in PyeongChang, their last appearance on the Olympic stage. Nothing had been left to chance. Scott and Tessa wanted to show up in South Korea with the feeling that they had done all they could and be able to say, "We're ready."

I can confirm that they were indeed ready. I witnessed two athletes on a mission. The work had paid off, as they became Olympic gold medalists for the second time on February 20, 2018.

Scott and Tessa were *students of the game*. This expression refers to an intrinsic thirst for knowledge, a need to continually seek opportunities to grow and improve. Students of the game gather piles of information from their experts so they can show up at a competition certain that they've done everything to achieve the hoped-for outcome. These types of performers know that if you want to fill your toolbox, you have to want to open it first. Well, to learn just about anything, first you need to open your mind. You must *choose* to become your own best coach.

The key to success

In 2015, an elite sports academy in Luxembourg invited me to give a talk to staff and students. The first thing that struck me when I walked into the main gymnasium was an enormous vertical banner on which the following was written:

$$\mathsf{K}\, eep$$
$$\mathsf{E}\, ducating$$
$$\mathsf{Y}\, ourself$$

What a powerful message for teenagers! Student athletes and staff members couldn't help but notice the poster as they walked by it every day. It was the school motto. Their unwavering attention and numerous questions during my talk blew me away; it confirmed their thirst for learning. After this experience, I, too, drew inspiration from this acronym, not only for my own self-improvement but also to help my clients during coaching sessions.

Elite athletes are masters of the KEY philosophy. They're hungry for knowledge day after day, even if the lessons learned are small. They carefully gather all the information that can help them improve. Oftentimes, it's the tiny details that can translate into shaving a few milliseconds off their time, and milliseconds can make the difference in getting on the podium or not. Small things can have a big impact. Think about that little drop of water dripping into the sink. It's practically nothing, yet powerful enough to catch your attention and bug the heck out of you! Well, little gains on the playing field can have the same significant impact.

Mikaël Kingsbury is another exceptional learner. At the age of 28, this moguls skier is both a gold and a silver Olympic medalist. He's won nine Crystal Globes, the trophy awarded annually to the best freestyle skier in the world. He's stepped onto the podium 91 times in 109 World Cup starts. Of these, he's climbed to the top of the podium 63 times. Did I mention that he is also a four-time world champion? Yeah, no wonder his nickname is the King!

During one of our sessions, I asked Mik why he so completely dominated his sport. Why isn't there someone else like him? My questions caught him a bit off guard, so he thought about it for a few seconds, then answered.

First, Mik replied, "No one is as obsessed about the details as I am." It's true. Mik carefully analyzes each of his opponents' runs while waiting for his turn.

Second, he added, "I make it a point to learn a little something new each day. I like to go to bed at night knowing that I'm better than I was when I woke up in the morning." Once again, it's so true. He finds a way to lift a little more weight than the last time. He becomes stronger. He adjusts the position of his ankles while zipping down the moguls course. He becomes faster. He makes sure that he takes away something new during each of the mental training sessions. He becomes more confident.

Mik is always looking for opportunities to learn. He loves every challenge I throw at him: big or small, he never backs away from them. He *wants* to be challenged, because challenges are opportunities that have to be seized.

> Success isn't based on luck. Success comes down to a limitless desire to learn. Great athletes understand that being successful isn't about measuring up to others. It's all about measuring up to yourself.

The experience of learning

The concept of *having experience* deserves some thought.

Many individuals believe that just exposing themselves to different situations and work environments over the years invariably leads to learning important lessons, making them better at what they do. This isn't exactly the case. The best learning experiences happen when we have clear intentions. Purposeful, intentional, and meaningful goals will help us really progress.

At work, we constantly talk about the importance of having experience. For example, we may say that a person has thirty years of experience in their field. What does this mean exactly? If the experience we're talking about is repeating the same routine day in, day out, without feeling engaged and with no clear intentions, what value does it really have?

In contrast, another candidate may have no more than ten years' experience; if this career path is the product of a well-thought-out approach based on clear intentions and reaching specific goals, we're talking about a purposeful working experience that may carry more value than that of someone who's been at it three times as long.

Most of the people who operate according to strategic learning principles are fans of self-assessment and peer feedback. A participant at one of my talks was wondering how to get better at leading important meetings. I suggested that he film his next boardroom meeting and analyze it afterward, just like athletes do with video sessions after games. Video doesn't lie; it tells the cold, hard truth! The answers are self-evident, and what we learn from video analysis is priceless. If you've never watched yourself perform, it may lead to vulnerable feelings, but hey, getting out of your comfort zone is what becoming an Olympian at work is all about.

Don't get me wrong, you can still evolve if you go about your business with a punch-in and punch-out approach, but if you truly want to grow quickly and become a high-performer at work, then the purposeful experience approach is the way to go.

Having experience is a fairly arbitrary concept. In the end, personal development is mostly based on *what we gain* from our experiences, rather than just gaining experience, and our ability to use the lessons learned to improve our skills.

Even the King makes mistakes

Let's turn back the clock a little. It's January 2017, and we're in Lake Placid for the FIS Freestyle Ski World Cup. This picturesque village in upstate New York also hosted the 1932 and 1980 Olympic Games.

It was Friday the thirteenth (no, I'm not superstitious), and the men's moguls event was about to take place. Mikaël Kingsbury dominated the international circuit at the time.

Mikaël had podiumed during every World Cup since March 2014. He was on fire, so his goal was to keep this impressive streak alive. He started the day with a bang, zipping down the course with laser-like precision during his qualifying run. Everything had been going well up to that point.

Then came the final round. Six competitors remained. Mik was one run away from another victory. His game plan was to keep his hips forward, control his speed, and let his skis do the rest. He was waiting for his turn when American Bradley Wilson pushed off. As expected, the home crowd went crazy. Carried along by his American fans, Wilson ripped through the course with blistering speed. The judges were impressed and rewarded the local favorite with a big score, putting Wilson temporarily in first place. Kingsbury was perfectly aware that the American had put down a remarkable run that was going to be hard to beat. Usually Mik stays cool and collected in this kind of situation. Not this time.

Overcome with emotion, Mik pushed his game plan aside and attacked the course with a vengeance. Bad idea. He made a few uncharacteristic mistakes and finished sixth. It was his worst result since another sixth-place finish in Lake Placid three years earlier, almost to the day.

Over the days that followed, Mik and I discussed at length what had happened. He came to the conclusion that he hadn't been focusing on the right thing. He had let his ego take over — "I'll show him who's the King" — instead of sticking to the established game plan. We reviewed some important lessons so he could approach this kind of situation differently in future.

Well, the future arrived a lot faster than anticipated. During the following weekend, another World Cup was taking place at Val Saint-Côme in Quebec. Mik found himself in almost the same situation, but this time, the King of moguls skiing was ready to face some adversity and keep his ego in check.

This time, Mikaël stayed true to his game plan to reach the top step on the podium. The local favorite was greeted by family and friends to celebrate his bounce-back victory. That's all Mikaël needed to kick off another impressive streak. Between the Val Saint-Côme World Cup (January 2017) and the PyeongChang Games (February 2018), Mikaël competed in sixteen World Cups; he won fourteen gold and two silver medals. An ideal preparation for the Olympic Games!

Events sometimes have a funny way of turning out. It's January 2019, Marie and I were drafting this anecdote, and my phone started ringing. My screen displayed *Mikaël Kingsbury*. Marie and I were blown away. What a coincidence! I picked up. "JF, it's Mik. I just finished my race. I screwed up. I wasn't focused enough. I caught my ski on a mogul and I finished fifth." He had just competed in a World Cup in Lake Placid of all places. Let's just say upstate New York isn't Mik's favorite place!

The student of the game went to work; Mik reflected, analyzed, and fine-tuned his skills. He made the necessary adjustments to succeed again. The following weekend, he won another World Cup in Mont-Tremblant, Quebec. Two weeks later, he achieved his season goal by winning two gold medals at the World Championships in Deer Valley, Utah. The King had bounced back once again.

This anecdote illustrates exactly what I mean by learning in a purposeful way. Mikaël's experience in Lake Placid was a milestone, and his intention to make it a turning point was clear. This is what purposeful learning is all about: experience that leads to important lessons that can be applied to making yourself better.

When you're not performing to your own expectations, ask yourself, "Why? What happened?" just like elite athletes do.

There's no point in criticizing yourself too much. By remaining objective, you'll focus instead on the details that explain your poor performance and come up with solutions to bounce back.

Forget about operating on autopilot

Autopilot is practical for aircrafts and ships. The system corrects the course automatically when the vehicles deviate from their routes.

Humans don't have an equivalent system to bring themselves back on course when they start to drift. Correcting their trajectory requires voluntary, not automatic, self-awareness and introspection. We'll come back to this in greater detail in Chapter 6, "Develop an Olympian Calm."

Athletes never rely on autopilot. They never settle for status quo or take the easy route. It's quite the opposite, as they want their training to be difficult and challenging. Athletes don't need someone else telling them to improve; they create their own opportunities to learn.

Because of the repetitive nature of training, athletes can easily choose to switch to autopilot. Every day, they go to the gym, meet their coaches, and repeat some of the same exercises. It's the same for workers. Every day, they show up at the office, cross paths with the same colleagues, and pick up their duties where they left off.

Cirque du Soleil performers also understand the danger of routine. Some perform up to 475 times in a year, doing the same choreography, dressed in the same costume, and performing the same act in the same theater.

Of all the artists I've coached at Cirque du Soleil, the clowns were my favorite performers to work with. Clowns are the heart and soul of the show, and most of them have fascinating life stories. They're arguably the most brilliant and creative, as well as wisest human beings I've ever met. If you ever have the chance to have lunch or grab a drink with a clown, do it!

The one clown who impressed me the most always avoided being in his comfort zone.

"I've watched you perform several times over the years, and, each time, I found that you were better than the last time," I once said to him. "The pleasure that you portray on stage is palpable; it's like it's always your first show. How do you do this when you perform the same show every night?"

"You're wrong," he replied. I was thrown for a loop by this answer. "I never do the same show twice, because the people who come to see me are always different. New crowd, new show!"

"What are you trying to say exactly?"

"Listen, JF. When I go to pick people out of the crowd to join me onstage, I force myself not to choose those who are ready to jump out of their seat. I make a point of picking those who are going to be a challenge. I have to improvise to find the right way to convince them to follow me onstage."

No wonder he was such an amazing performer. The important lesson here is to challenge yourself and leave your comfort zone if you want to excel. This particular clown was never afraid of becoming vulnerable, not even in front of a full house. Vulnerability opens the door to new experiences.

To become an Olympian at work, it's not enough to just put in the time and hope to evolve quickly. You need to take personal initiative and make a conscious effort to continue to learn. Below are a few examples:

- Read a book that will add a tool that is missing from your toolbox, such as a new communication skill.
- Take a course on a subject that excites you, such as learning to speak another language, to sew or cook, or to understand the stock market.
- Join a discussion group for professionals in your field to share with, learn from, and support each other.
- Improve your breathing technique to better face a stressful situation, such as managing a complex file at work.
- Register for a seminar to become technologically savvy.

No one wants to be the employee *who had so much potential*. On the contrary. You want to be the one who embraces their potential. Athletes *choose* to work daily at getting better. If you want to become an Olympian at work, you have to choose to seize every opportunity to become a valuable asset for your employer.

As a mental coach, I constantly remind my clients to find projects that make them "vibrate." Basically, any activities that sparks excitement while helping them develop and making them happy. Athletes take pleasure in their search for excellence. They *play* their sport. Don't be afraid to change your routine and do the things you like to do. Tennis on weekends. A movie on Tuesday evenings. A coffee with a friend on Sundays. Happy hour with a friend on Wednesdays. These spurts of pleasure will have a positive influence on different aspects of your life, including at work. So, get out there and vibrate!

Curiosity: a secret weapon

Antoine Valois-Fortier is one of the most accomplished judokas in the world. His obsession with details sets him apart from the others. When he was in high school, he would hide during study period and watch past world championships and Olympic Games on VHS. He knew the content of each cassette by heart. He is a true student of the game. Ask him who won gold at the World Championships of 1993, 2001, or 2007, and he'll list the names in a single go, without hesitation.

Elite athletes are curious creatures, always looking to reach new heights. Their quest for gold is an adventure into the unknown, like a treasure hunt.

As the saying goes, you don't have to be sick to get better. Top athletes don't wait to be weak to get stronger or until they are slow to become faster. It's about getting better regardless of where they are in the process of reaching their goals.

We shouldn't feel this urge to learn only when we have to solve a problem at work. We should feel it well in advance. Your process needs to become proactive. You may argue that it's important to know our flaws and weaknesses. You're right. We have to know ourselves well enough to identify what needs fine-tuning, and we must be humble enough to take action to address these deficiencies.

For example, you acknowledge not having given a colleague your full attention during yesterday's meeting. You also notice that this happens more often than you'd like. You could easily brush it off and move on because it's not a big deal, but you realize this behavior isn't optimal for team success. So, you decide to address the situation by apologizing and by challenging yourself to pay closer attention to what she's saying in future. Responding like this demands personal introspection, discipline, and humility. You take responsibility for your actions and decide to respond positively to improve on the situation. The word respons-ibility says it all: it's the *ability* to be *responsible*.

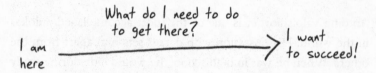

I am here ————————————> I want to succeed!

What do I need to do to get there?

Unlike the body, which slows down as we get older, the brain is designed to evolve over time, so it can continue to get stronger and smarter late into our lives.

I hugely admire people in their senior years who are in tip-top mental and physical shape. You know them. They're almost eighty, they have a spark in their eyes, muscular calves, and energy to spare. I love chatting with them to understand how they stay in such great shape. One energetic senior once told me, "JF, the day you stop challenging yourself is the day you start to die. I have a bunch of friends who have been dead for a long time."

> What's better:
> adding years to your life or adding life to your years?
> I'll leave you to think about that.

My clients who are workplace Olympians go about their business with a state of mind called *kaizen* ("kai" meaning change, and "zen" meaning better or best). This Japanese expression refers to a series of small improvements made in tiny, continuous doses. Ultimately, *curiosity* is the secret weapon that most high performers utilize to be able to live a kaizen lifestyle.

Being solid on your feet

You get my point. To evolve we have to challenge ourselves, like the Cirque du Soleil clown and Olympic athletes do. However, to get there, we have to see performance as a whole. To illustrate the principle, let's use your office desk as a metaphor.

To be able to perform under challenging circumstances, an athlete has to consider every aspect of their performance in order to be balanced, sturdy, and stable, so to speak. If one of the four training components (technical, tactical, physical, and mental) is neglected, they'll be unbalanced, in the same way a desk is unbalanced if one leg is shorter than the others. The same principle applies to the Olympian at work.

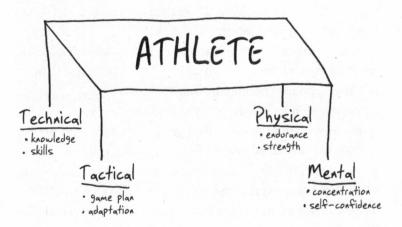

You can have the most specialized knowledge (technical), you may come up with the best sales strategy (tactical), you may feel you're in shape and well rested (physical), but you won't succeed if you don't have the proper mental skills to stay calm and be confident when under pressure. You won't be solid on your feet.

In the world of elite sports, successful athletes typically have the full package. Their desk has four long legs. It's practical for workers to go about their overall skills training the same way.

Do things right!

"Just try your best!" We hear this all the time. But what does it mean exactly? The statement suggests that the result to be achieved isn't clear, which leaves some room to error.

A colleague was telling me that his boss had once written an important letter that was full of spelling mistakes and addressed to the wrong person. Unacceptable, wouldn't you say? He was clearly in a rush and simply wanted to get it done quickly. Therefore, he certainly had no intention of writing a letter by the book and being respectful of its recipient. Simply trying to do his best was clearly not good enough.

When we do things in a careless manner and cut corners because we want to save a few minutes, we have to ask ourselves how much time we would need to correct our mistakes and make things right. Is it really worth it in the end?

Every national sports organization has a clear mission: to shoot for the podium at the Olympic and the Paralympic Games. In Canada, prior to hosting the 2010 Vancouver Olympic Games, an organization known as Own the Podium was created to help sports organizations describe their *gold medal profile*. This profile outlines the precise skills athletes will require to become champions in their discipline. This profile is then used by organizations to develop detailed yearly training programs, also known as YTPs. These twelve-month plans indicate what each athlete should be doing from one week to the next in order to peak at the right (Olympic) time. Each training session has its purpose. We ensure that everything has its purpose so that nothing is left to chance. The Olympics take place every four years, so it would be risky to settle for just trying to do our best.

In the workplace, most organizations define their company mission, vision, values, and goals for the year. Why doesn't an employee do the same thing by creating their own gold medal profile for work?

Defining a clear game plan with strategic checkpoints along the way is key to achieving career goals. Ask any Olympian what lies ahead in the coming year. Believe me, they'll know. And if they were to ask you the same question, would you be able to explain your own YTP?

We rarely think to ask ourselves, "What did I do today that will help boost my career?" Clear and precise intentions are the principles that guide us throughout our professional development and ensure that our daily actions have a real impact on our ultimate goals.

"Delicious uncertainty"

Every day at training, an Olympic athlete is working to improve, whether technically, tactically, physically, or mentally. Daily goals could include things like

- moving faster,
- listening better to the coach's feedback; or
- perfecting conscious breathing between sets.

Oftentimes, the athlete writes these daily goals in a journal, discusses them with their coach before practice sessions, and goes back to the notes again during practice, if needed.

You can use a similar method at work. For example, a client of mine, the CEO of a small tech company, uses the first ten minutes of his day at the office to write what he calls his reminders for improvement. Below are a few of them:

- speak to each of my employees
- take short breaks (maximum time without a break: ninety minutes)
- be selfish and protect my schedule (say no to demands that will eat up my time)

These reminders appear on his desktop for the day. Out of sight, out of mind, right? Well, for this corporate leader, it became *within sight, within mind*.

Paying attention to details does not guarantee success. In fact, Olympians deal with failure more often than triumph. This may seem paradoxical, but it's true.

Let's say that if an Olympian sets goals that are well below their skill level, the likelihood that they'll achieve them is very high. However, their level of satisfaction will be low. You don't become an Olympic champion by setting easy goals. Becoming a champion requires getting out of your comfort zone through tough training conditions. The athlete wants to feel vulnerable and suffer pain, key components of self-growth.

To get the best out of your employees as a corporate leader, you have to put them to the test by demanding neither too little nor too much, but just enough. You need to find their sweet spot. To be able to do this well, a manager must assess employees' skill sets and detect where they are in their progression, just like a sports coach does with their athletes. This process then helps determine the best challenges to set for each of them.

For instance, if you ask an experienced and well-trained employee to tackle an easy challenge, they'll get bored. If you ask an inexperienced worker who lacks self-confidence to undertake a highly complex challenge, they'll become anxious. But if you suggest a challenge that perfectly matches the employee's skill level, they'll be motivated and excited to carry out the task. Eventually, these challenges will help the employee maximize their potential.

This approach is based on a model developed in 1988 by Dr. Jean Brunelle and his colleagues called *délicieuse incertitude*, or delicious uncertainty. Essentially, it's all about getting the learner into a sweet spot that comes from being challenged just enough.

I use this conceptual model regularly in my coaching to ensure that my clients steadily progress in their development. Good

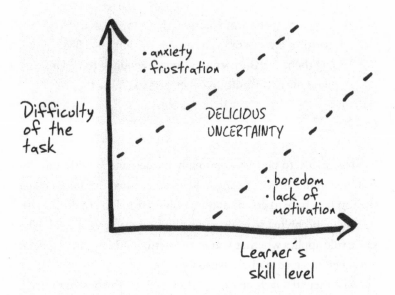

leaders know how to get their employees going. It's a subtle skill that isn't always easy to put into practice. It can take a significant amount of time, trial, and error before it can be used correctly, but in the end, when the employee is regularly operating in their ideal learning zone, their development can skyrocket, and all the effort to get to this place can be rewarded.

Are you disciplined?

Five birds are perched on an electric wire and all of them decide to fly away. How many are left? Five. They decided to leave but didn't actually do it!

Do you see yourself in this joke?

Everyone is looking to improve in one area or another. But there's a difference between *deciding* to do something and actually *doing* it. Many people fail because they simply aren't able to apply the required discipline. You're not alone.

> Discipline is the state of mind that motivates us to perform a series of tasks, even if we don't feel like doing them. It's the mental strength required to tackle mundane or difficult tasks because we know they're key to our success.

The ability to perform optimally on demand is fairly rare. In fact, becoming an elite in any field is rather uncommon. To reach the top, you have to go about things differently, look to distinguish yourself, and be ready to do more than others in your field. The same rule applies whether you're an Olympic athlete, an engineer, a teacher, or an administrative assistant.

As a mental coach, my mandate is to help the best athletes in the world to thrive. My philosophy is that if you work with high performers, you need to be a high performer yourself. The way I see it, I don't deserve to work with these incredible human beings if I don't push myself to be the best I can be. Otherwise, what credibility would I have when I ask these athletes to push their limits if I don't challenge myself?

My mission for the PyeongChang 2018 Olympic Games in South Korea was to help the athletes win gold medals. It was as simple as that. I had plenty of time to think about this mission during my fifteen-hour flight to Seoul!

People who go to the Olympic Games will tell you that it's like running a marathon. It's true. I was in PyeongChang for twenty-four days, coaching seven athletes competing in five different sports, with no days off. Half of them were competing in the mountains, and the other half in the city. I had to switch accommodations five times so that I could be close to the athletes and coaches.

At home, I work four days a week and enjoy long weekends to spend time with family and friends, get some extra rest, and do my favorite hobbies. In PyeongChang, I had to be *on* all the time in a continuously changing environment with the pressure at its pinnacle, given the magnitude of the Olympic Games.

During the last few weeks leading up to the Games, I reminded myself that if the athletes had to be perfectly prepared, I did, too. So, I decided to purposefully go to bed early several nights a week to accumulate some additional rest. I also drew up a specific game plan in anticipation of the twenty-four-day marathon.

Upon arrival, I put my game plan into action with intense discipline. I was in the gym at 6:00 every morning. All my meals were planned to provide my body with the energy it needed until bedtime. I took time every day after lunch to nap or meditate — *me time* that allowed me to recover from the morning's fatigue and build up stamina for the rest of the day. I made sure to get my beauty sleep every night. I was on a mission.

There were moments when I found my game plan to be routine and rigid. How many times did I resist the temptation to go to bed later so that I could cheer on Canadian athletes competing in other sports? After all, I was at the Olympics, wasn't I? Not to mention the times I would have willingly swapped my balanced meals for more delicious comfort food options. Try resisting the tempting smell of burgers when you walk next to the Golden Arches three times a day. Yes, you guessed it: there was a McDonald's in the Olympic cafeteria. Not cool for the athletes' menus, eh? But what can you do? The Olympics have a large appetite for sponsorship money. Each time the temptation would arise, I would go back to the heart of the matter: Why are you here, JF? *To help the athletes achieve their dreams.* This short reminder was enough to bring me back to my mission.

In hindsight, I'm convinced that this robust discipline played a key role in helping me do my job at a high level throughout the Games. I was able to maintain my upbeat energy, be attentive to the athletes' needs, and stay focused during the entire run. I never crashed.

The athletes I was coaching won several medals. What impact did *my* performance have on these results? We'll never know. What I do know, though, is that I offered the best version of myself.

My performance in PyeongChang was based on a few of the important factors mentioned in Chapter 1:

- I chose to be my own teacher (*student of the game*) thanks to a well-thought-out preparation plan that I executed to a T.
- I drew a lot from previous eventful experiences courtesy of the Rio Games in 2016.
- I arrived in South Korea with *clear intentions* and *daily reminders* to stay focused.
- I provided myself with the means to remain *balanced*. My table had four very sturdy legs.

Seize every opportunity to learn. Be proactive. If you become the master of your own progress, you'll become an Olympian at whatever your area of expertise.

In the following chapters, we'll discuss several concepts that will help you perform on demand, deal with complex situations, believe in your own abilities, and remain calm under pressure.

CHAPTER 2

Dream Big

The results of a major Gallup poll published in the United States in 2017 on employee engagement at work are pretty alarming. The third edition of the *State of the American Workplace* reveals that a mere 33 percent of American workers love their jobs, while 51 percent are not engaged at work at all — they're only doing what's necessary — and the remaining 16 percent are completely disengaged and feel terrible at work.

These days, motivational speakers and various types of life coaches are increasingly in demand. Some companies are devoting large sums of money to use their services. If they feel that their employees need to learn strategies to increase motivation and engagement at work, it only means one thing: there is clearly a need!

Since 2013, I've given hundreds of keynote speeches on this very topic. I spend a lot of time talking with workers at different companies in various industries and I've noticed the same thing with my own eyes: very few people are actually happy at work. This worries me. This is an example in which the difference between the workplace and the sports world is strikingly obvious. Most athletes feel so passionate about their sport and are fully committed to it. The ones who don't feel this way are the exception.

What makes athletes feel that way? How do they keep that passion for their sport despite the heartbreaking losses, the injuries, and the sacrifices they make?

Let's take a closer look to find out.

Where does motivation come from?

The word motivation is derived from the Latin word *movere*, meaning "to move." It's the engine that drives us to do something. Defining and understanding what fuels our motivation and how it relates to our life goals is really important.

Here's a memory aid. Let's split the word motivation: *motiv* means reason, while *-ation*, refers to action. Motivation is basically the sum of the reasons that make us take action.

You may already know that there are two types of motivation: intrinsic (internal) and extrinsic (external). Intrinsic motivation lies inside each of us. For example:

- the love for your job,
- the passion for the profession you've chosen,
- the desire to change,
- having a curious mind,
- feeling useful; and
- knowing you made a difference.

Extrinsic motivation comes from external sources, including

- money,
- peer recognition,
- energy conveyed by colleagues,
- promotions,
- children, friends, and colleagues; and
- medals and awards.

Which is the most important: intrinsic or extrinsic? Which one should we prioritize? From experience, I've noticed both types of motivation can drive us to act and to excel.

And yet, if I were to ask you which of them would last the longest and have the greatest impact on our lives, without a doubt, the answer would be intrinsic motivation. It's not the medal that motivates an Olympian the most. It's the journey, the improvements, and reaching the goals they've set for themself. I see the same thing among workers.

There is one major difference that sets these two types of motivation apart: we completely control our intrinsic motivation but we have no control over extrinsic motivators. If we could set our own pay grade, all of us would give ourselves a raise, right? Unfortunately, it doesn't work that way! In contrast, only *we* can control our level of enthusiasm and passion.

So you may think that all we need is intrinsic motivation. Well, not really. My experience has shown that both types are necessary to achieve optimal motivation, and it's best to use all available sources. It's fine to be motivated by money or your boss's praise, but we can't be motivated by external factors only. We have little control over the salaries we earn and the feedback coming from our boss, even if we're convinced that we did a good job and we deserve some additional recognition. When extrinsic motivation is greater than intrinsic motivation, we are *not* the primary source of our impetus for improvement. As a result, we have little control over the situation.

In an ideal world, you want to be both intrinsically and extrinsically motivated, giving a slight upper hand to internal motivators. For example, let's take an employee that feels valued through their high salary (extrinsic), the recognition of their peers (extrinsic), and the bonus to which they feel entitled (extrinsic). If they were counting on these three factors alone to feed their motivation, they would quickly feel unmotivated if the company didn't pay the bonus at the end of the year. On the other hand, if

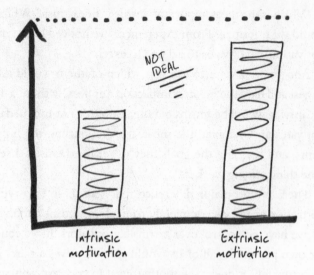

NOT IDEAL

Intrinsic motivation   Extrinsic motivation

this employee were to say to themselves every day how much they love their job (intrinsic), are proud of achieving the goals that they had set for themselves (intrinsic), are eager to continue to improve (intrinsic), and they *didn't* get the bonus they were counting on, they would certainly be disappointed but would accept the situation and move on.

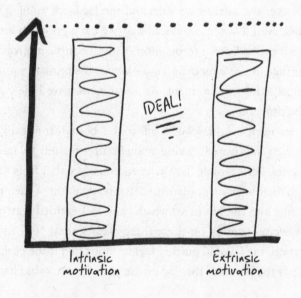

IDEAL!

Intrinsic motivation   Extrinsic motivation

> If intrinsic and extrinsic motivators were to come to blows, intrinsic would almost always win. It's simply stronger.

Of course, high-level athletes get excited about the prize money, the sponsorships, the medals, and the recognition of others. However, I make sure that their intrinsic motivation prevails. It's a proven recipe for success.

Sometimes, it just feels good

Occasionally, we deviate from our intrinsic motivators in favor of extrinsic motivators, which can bring mixed results. Here's a story that a professor shared with us while I was studying sports psychology at university.

Roger earned a living as a manager in a manufacturing company. He always made it his mission to know his employees well. He knew their career and personal goals, as well as what got them going on a daily basis. He was well aware of the power and the pitfalls of the different types of motivation.

Now retired, Roger lives in a country village where everyone knows him. Behind his beautiful home lies a huge yard in which he planted a vegetable garden, his latest passion. One beautiful afternoon, he arrived home from running errands to find a group of neighborhood boys playing football next to his property. The end zone was located far too close to his vegetable garden for his liking. He told himself that the ball would inevitably end up in his plants. But Roger had the perfect strategy in mind to protect his property.

The boys were having a blast! They made some beautiful plays and were taking the game very seriously, focused as if the Vince Lombardi Trophy were on the line. Time stood still. Roger approached them, his vegetable garden top of mind. At first, the boys were a little uncomfortable, thinking that they had offended their elderly neighbor. Roger, who looked cool, calm, and collected, asked them how long they had been there. "Two hours," one of them said. The conversation then went something like this.

"So, you're having fun?" Roger asked.

"You bet! We made some amazing plays!" they said. The boys were bursting with excitement. Roger, still worried about his plants, began to roll out his strategy.

"So, how about coming back tomorrow at noon. I'll give you each $2 for the show. How does that sound?"

The boys were surprised, yet even more motivated to come back the next day. They showed up at 12:00 p.m. sharp. At this point, the boys were driven by internal *and* external sources of motivation. Roger was sitting comfortably on his patio, watching the boys having some fun. Forty-five minutes later, the boys decided that they had played enough and were curious to know if this story about getting paid was for real.

"So, did you have fun?" Roger asked.

"Yeah . . . what d'ya think? Are we still good for the two dollars?" they wondered.

"Of course!" said Roger, who proceeded to give cash to each of the boys. He then asked, "Why did you only play for forty-five minutes today?"

"No reason," they chimed.

"Well, then, I'll see you tomorrow and, this time, there'll be a five-dollar bill for each of you!"

The boys were happy and gave each other high fives. "Retired people are awesome!" they thought. Of course, they showed up the next day as planned. Before the game, Roger heard them talking about what they were going to buy with their seven dollars. But this time, the boys played half-heartedly for no more than twenty-five minutes.

"Hey, mister! Are we good for the five dollars?"

Roger gave them each the agreed amount. "Why did you only play for twenty-five minutes today?" he asked.

"No reason," they replied.

"Okay. So, you'll come back at the same time tomorrow?"

They quickly did the math. After receiving two dollars, then five, they thought the third game might be even more lucrative.

"Sure," they confirmed.

"Perfect. So, tomorrow, it'll be one dollar each," Roger explained.

"Why just one dollar?" they wondered.

"No reason," Roger said.

Well, needless to say, the boys never came back, and Roger's tomatoes grew undisturbed.

Roger's strategy was to change the boys' main source of motivation. They started out by playing behind Roger's property, driven by a very strong intrinsic motivation. They played for the pleasure of the game. When money entered into the equation, the initial motivation took a big hit and became secondary. For the boys, seven dollars represented a tidy sum of money. Roger's monetary reward carried a lot of weight in their decision whether to come back or not. When the amount to be won wasn't worth it, the boys were done with Roger.

You might think that Roger protected his vegetables in a somewhat questionable way. Fair enough. But, by doing so, he taught the boys an important lesson: extrinsic motivation can be a trap when it overshadows intrinsic motivation.

I've witnessed the same effect on professional athletes who sign multimillion-dollar contracts. Take the young, extremely talented hockey player who really goes all-out every game, simply because he's crazy about his sport. At some point, while still in his late teens, he gets drafted and eventually signs his first professional contract to the beautiful sound of *ka-ching, ka-ching*. Mission accomplished, as he says to himself, "Man, I've made it to the show!" In this world of young multimillionaires, watch out for extrinsic motivation: the luxury car, the media attention, the big bucks, the fancy restaurants, and the attractive women. All of a sudden, internal motivators, such as self-determination and perseverance, have to compete against enticing external motivators.

In the workplace, what should a manager do to rally their troops? What will encourage an employee to excel and reach their full potential? The easiest answer is to set goals, right? Goals mean having a game plan to follow, incorporating clear intentions, and, ultimately, moving forward. Have you heard of the acronym SMART? The five letters stand for specific, measurable, achievable, realistic, and timely. You might have heard this acronym over and over again, like a broken record.

Having a chance to feel optimally motivated all the time is more complex than only setting a series of goals. We're going to discuss this challenge in greater detail later in this chapter, but first, we need to talk about the importance of having great aspirations and ambitious dreams.

Is having dreams ludicrous?

Whether we're a parent, an aunt, or a grandfather, we all encourage children to use their imaginations, to dream big. What do you want to be when you grow up? A firefighter, an astronaut, a hockey player in the NHL, the president? Or perhaps a mental performance coach! As kids, we pin up posters of the people we admire on the walls of our bedrooms. We look at them daily. On Halloween, we certainly don't stop children from dressing up as a doctor, a police officer, or their favorite superhero. Talking about our wildest dreams is accepted, encouraged, even valued. As grown-ups, we love hearing kids talk about their vision of the future, whether we think it's strange or not.

In 2002, the whole world was watching the Olympic Games in Salt Lake City, including a nine-year-old boy living in Deux-Montagnes, Quebec, who took in the moguls skiing competition on television, his eyes glued to the screen in wonder. It was a moment that would forever change Mikaël Kingsbury's life. After getting the green light from his parents to take up freestyle skiing, he drew the Olympic rings on a piece of paper followed by the words *I will win*. He decided to stick it to the ceiling over his bed so that he could see it every morning when he woke up and every night when he went to sleep. He's now twenty-eight years old, an Olympic champion, and arguably the most dominant athlete in the world.

Mik was allowed to dream. He never felt embarrassed when his family and friends saw this crazy dream hanging over his bed. This ambitious goal had a major impact on his behavior, day in and day out. Great champions are champions in their minds before they become champions in reality. They think, act, and feel like winners all the time. Ultimately, Mik will tell you that his wildest dream at the age of nine had a significant impact in winning gold at the 2018 Olympics. And if he had never won Olympic gold, his commitment to his dream would have still allowed him to achieve great things, like his silver medal at the Sochi Games in 2014, his nine Crystal Globes, and his multiple world championship titles.

Have you noticed that once you became an adult, all of this seemed to disappear? As we age, we lose the ability to dream of achieving our deepest and most meaningful ambitions. When we reach adolescence, society stops encouraging this kind of behavior, and adults begin transmitting messages asking us to be serious. "What? You want to become a circus artist? Come on, stop dreaming and get a real job!" It gets even worse once we're adults. We're embarrassed to verbalize our aspirations for fear of being judged and appearing unrealistic.

As a result, many of us end up following the "prescribed" professional path, which is neither exciting nor rewarding.

We march on like automatons and simply live routine lives, often due to strong extrinsic motivation. We abandon our dreams.

Dreaming won't hurt you

Before we go any further, I would like to address the differences between a dream and a fantasy. A fantasy is light, a little utopian, and not necessarily a serious goal. It can brighten our day, but it isn't a starting point like a dream is.

A dream is built from ambition, the willingness to accomplish something that will make us feel fulfilled. It gives our lives a direction. The thought of achieving our dreams ignites excitement and motivates us to push through the tough challenges.

In contrast to children, most adults avoid setting any sort of ambitious dreams for two reasons: the fear of failing and the fear of being judged.

Their inner monologue would sound something like this: "Oh no, I can't aim that high. If my dream doesn't come true, I'll have failed. What will people think? This is even worse than not having had a dream at all."

Children don't think like that. They don't care. At age eight, I was so sure that I was going to play for the Montreal Canadiens despite my hockey skills being good but not amazing. As things turned out, I didn't play for the Habs, but I feel that my sports dream has taken me just as far.

To paraphrase Benjamin Franklin, "Nothing is certain, except death and taxes." Of course, just because we have a dream doesn't mean we can make it come true. Yet all the Olympians I've had the pleasure to get to know proved one thing: you have to *dream big* if you want to achieve something big. If all the athletes that dreamed of winning an Olympic gold medal had first calculated the chances of that happening, I'm not sure the Olympic Games would even exist.

Take a moment to think about your own life. Can you think of one or two big dreams that you cherish as an adult? Do you have any at all? If you don't, think about getting some. Choose a life goal that will make you proud; whether you think it's achievable or not doesn't matter right now. And if this ambitious dream doesn't scare you, it's not big enough. Think of something else. Got one? Give it a shot, and let time dictate where your dream takes you. You'll soon realize that the sky's the limit.

If you haven't identified that dream yet, take the time you need to keep thinking about it until you settle on something, then keep on reading.

For many years during the first half of the twentieth century, people thought that the mile couldn't be run in under four minutes. On May 6, 1954, Roger Bannister of Great Britain changed everyone's minds with a time of 3 minutes, 59 seconds, and 4 one-hundredths of a second. The previous record of 4 minutes, 1 second, and 4 one-hundredths of a second had stood for nine years. Only forty-six days later, Bannister's record was broken. Other runners thought, "Hey, he did it, so why not me?" Today, the quickest time recorded for a mile is almost seventeen seconds faster than Bannister's initial feat. That's what it means to dream big!

The word *impossible* can tarnish our intentions and inhibit positive thinking. The real go-getters, however, see that word differently. With a little tinkering, *impossible* can become *I'm possible*. The shift in thinking between *impossible* and *I'm possible* is a choice. All those who ran the mile in less than four minutes chose the second option.

Big dreams have an impact on our daily behavior, our choices, and the way we see life. They can also affect the people we choose to have around us. Keeping a dream alive in our daily lives has been proven to be an excellent antidote to the factors that work against it.

An obsessive dream-goal works like an icebreaker; it creates its own path in spite of the obstacles

Despite his small stature, former hockey superstar Martin St. Louis proved to the skeptics that his dream of playing in the National Hockey League was possible. He kept telling himself, "I'll show you," when so many said he wouldn't make it. Well, "I'll show you" became "I told you so." Such a great feeling!

During my master's program in sports psychology, I had to give a presentation to defend my summer internship, the last assignment to conclude my graduate degree. The professors on the jury asked us to explain where we saw ourselves in ten years. Most students in the program gave politically correct answers. The way I interpreted the question was, "Tell us, Jean François, what are your ultimate dream goals that you want to achieve in the next decade?" In all seriousness, I replied that I would work for a well-known sports organization that was recognized internationally, and I would also work with at least one elite athlete who would become the best in the world. I can still see their reaction. Only one professor looked at me with a big, approving smile on his face. The others were stunned and probably thought I was pretentious or arrogant. In my mind, I was only explaining what I *truly* wanted to achieve, with no pretension at all.

Committing leads to perseverance

Motivation is the spark that sets things in motion, but if you want it to take you to greater heights, *commitment* will get you there. Being motivated on its own is not enough. The parent who gets up in the middle of the night because his little baby is crying is not necessarily motivated to get out of his comfortable bed. It's his commitment to his child that gives him the willpower to do it, night after night.

The power of commitment is the same for the Olympian and the individual at work. If Mikaël Kingsbury had abandoned his dream of being an Olympic champion after his silver medal in Sochi in 2014, he would never have experienced the utter magic of his victory four years later in PyeongChang. Committing to his dream transformed his silver medal, seemingly a failure, into a launch pad to aim higher.

Below are a few questions to help you determine your level of motivation at work:

- Is it easy to find the motivation to carry out the tasks that require extra effort?
- Do you feel inspired when you walk into the office in the morning to face the day's challenges?
- Do you regularly have moments of excitement at work? When? What causes this excitement?
- Are you really committed and ready to do whatever it takes to tackle your duties?

Strategies to feed your motivation

There are a number of strategies to increase your level of motivation, and I would like to share a few that have worked well for elite performers and leaders in the workplace I've coached over the years.

The minimum principle

Taking your time is more powerful than you may think. In today's society, we want everything done quickly. We want to look and feel better, fast. Let's take New Year's resolutions as an example. "This year, I'm going to lose twenty-five pounds. I know it'll work this time!" You haven't exercised in five years? No problem. Here we go, let's hit the gym hard five times a week. It's all or nothing! Sound familiar? At that rate, you'll be lucky to make it to March.

A few years ago, a business client used my services to help him manage the pressure he was experiencing at work. After a few sessions, he said, "JF, I have another problem I want to solve.

My doctor told me that I have to lose a few pounds. Can you help me lose weight quickly?" As we all know, losing weight can be a psychological challenge.

I could see that my client was in a hurry, so I decided to push things a little further. When I asked him if he thought that he could work out five times a week, his answer was a definite *no*.

I continued. "How many sessions per week do you think will be necessary to start the process?" He gave a typical response: three.

So, I suggested, "And if I were to say two times?" It wasn't enough. I then explained that, in fact, if we compared it to five times per week, it's true, it's not very much. But if we compared it to nothing for the last five years, two is pretty good, isn't it? I saw that my client was starting to understand what I was getting at. So I went even further. "What if you went to the gym once this week? That's more than what you've done in the last few weeks, isn't it? You'll still be ahead, right?" He couldn't disagree.

The minimum principle is a strategy that I learned from one of my colleagues, Joshua Seldman, a performance coach based in New York City. This principle helps *build momentum*, as they say in the sports world, so that you can maintain a certain pace with assurance and enthusiasm. It's also a question of perspective. If I go to the gym once during the week with the goal of only going once, then it's mission accomplished. On the other hand, if I go to the gym twice, with the goal of going five times, the likelihood of my giving up increases tenfold. Never underestimate the power of the minimums.

This principle works really well when you're facing a tough file at work. Sometimes you just have to give yourself the chance to start, after which the wheels will begin to turn and gather speed, leading to greater motivation.

Interactive self-motivation

One of my mentors would always say, "One of the best ways to motivate yourself is to motivate others." He was right. I've noticed this numerous times in my coaching. Let's look at this principle more closely.

It's early in the morning and outside it is rainy and cold. At the office, colleagues are complaining about the weather and whining about the overtime they'll have to work today to finish the project underway. And you feel the same way. Your own motivation is low, yet you understand that by changing your attitude, the day could be more enjoyable for you and your colleagues. You decide to turn things around. You purposefully get fired up and say to them, "Okay, everybody. If we tackle this like we know we can, we'll save some time. Remember the last time? We got through it despite a series of obstacles. Let's think about the end result and what we'll be giving our clients. Let's go!" Your colleagues are a little surprised, but they understand that it's in their interest to get going. You and your colleagues go back to your workstations, encouraged and collectively stoked. Your energy is contagious. By putting out energetic behaviors, even if you fake it at first, the positive vibe spreads quickly throughout the workplace and everyone gets to enjoy the stimulating feeling of endorphins. All of a sudden, the dreary morning just got a little brighter for everyone.

This strategy is especially useful for athletes that play team sports. For example, a hockey player on the bench realizes that he's lacking energy. He decides to give a tap on the shin pads of his teammates and shouts, "Don't give up, boys. One shift at a time (the minimum principle). We can do it!" In doing so, he not only increased his teammates' mojo, but his own as well.

Try this strategy at work. You'll see that it's effective and, best of all, easy to use.

180 degrees

Another method to stay motivated is to take the time to stop, turn 180 degrees, and take stock of the progress made in carrying out a project or a task. The 180 degrees tactic is handy when we're working on a complex and challenging file that might require some additional mental strength.

We have no problem looking ahead, right?

- What's on for tomorrow?
- When is the next meeting scheduled?
- What's on my calendar for next week?

Still, we're less likely to look back. And when we do, our thoughts are often drawn to the mistakes we made. Instead, train your brain to pay attention to the good stuff.

Progress
Achievements
Victories
----> Meetings
Projects
Deadlines

Paying particular attention to the progress made provides a sense of satisfaction that we wouldn't have otherwise. Then, when you think about the future, you end up looking at it differently. You become more inclined to attack the upcoming project. Writing down the achievements in a logbook for the duration of the project and occasionally reading them is one concrete way to remember the progress made.

Last summer, I embarked on an ambitious home project: renovating my kitchen. It took thirty-eight days straight. Before I started, I was fully aware of the magnitude of the challenge. I was apprehensive about reaching a point where I would be completely discouraged. Anyone who's undertaken this kind of project knows that there comes a time when we're fed up. Dust everywhere, loud banging sounds, and no kitchen access for several weeks. Oh, did I mention that I have two young kids? I'm not going to lie; I was a little stressed out! So, to avoid hitting the wall — no pun intended — I decided to test this motivation strategy. Each day, I set myself the challenge of finishing *at least* one task just by chipping away at it. I told myself that each completed task, big or small, was a step closer to the final outcome. Some days, it was a bigger step like installing the kitchen cabinets. Other days, it might only be installing a light fixture. The advantage was that, after each day, I could tell myself that I was a step ahead. Such a rewarding feeling! Just becoming aware of the daily progress was enough to avoid hitting the wall . . . and having access to a beautiful kitchen!

Knowing "why"

When people come to my office and say that their motivation is slipping, I often ask them *why* they do what they do.

- Why do you spend forty, fifty, or sixty hours at work?
- Why do you go to the gym five times a week?
- Why are you following a strict diet?

Reconnecting with the fundamental reasons that explain why we do our jobs can help reignite our inner drive.

A highly talented, fourteen-year-old hockey player was having a fantastic start to the season, but then got into a slump for a few weeks and needed some help to get out of it. Sitting in my office, sulking and slouching forward, he clearly looked like he didn't want to be there. I asked him how things were going, and he said in a monotonous tone, "Okay."

"So, I understand that you came to see me because you aren't very motivated to play hockey right now."

"Not really. Things are bad right now," he replied.

"If you had to rate your level of motivation right now on a scale of zero to ten, what would it be?"

"Two."

I'm not sure why, but clients never say zero.

"Two?" I replied with a smile, "So, you have some?"

"Yeah, but not enough," he said.

"You want more motivation, and I get it. It's normal. So, tell me one thing: why do you play hockey?"

He didn't see this question coming at all. In fact, I'm always shocked to see that even adults rarely ask themselves this important question. So, after thinking about it for a few seconds, the young player found his answer.

"Because I love it."

"Really? You love hockey right now?"

"Well, not really. Not that much."

"So, talk to me about what you loved about it then."

His body language still showed a certain weariness.

"Uh . . . well, scoring goals is pretty fun."

"Really, tell me more!" The boy went on about it. "Anything else?" I asked.

"When the crowd starts to cheer us on. When I do a body check. When I create sick plays. When I make the perfect pass. Spending time with the guys. When I work hard, and we win."

The boy's attitude had started to change. He suddenly sounded enthusiastic. His face revealed a new energy. Perched on the edge of his chair, he spoke easily. I then decided to come back to the rating.

"Okay, that's great. How would you rate it out of ten now?"

Knowing that he had fallen into a trap, he said, "seven."

The boy had gone from two to seven in a matter of mere minutes because he was able to go back to the fundamental reasons for why he was so passionate about hockey. He wrote his reasons down on a piece of paper that he carries in his hockey bag.

To help him snap out of his slump, I asked him to read his list of whys before training sessions and games.

Witnessing how useful the *why* was for my clients, I created my own. It says, *Today, I have the honor and the privilege of helping people achieve their dreams.*

I put it on my computer desktop so that I repeat it every morning before I start my day. I insist on telling myself how lucky I am to coach such exceptional people.

A Cirque du Soleil trapeze artist will tell herself before every show, "The audience members experience strong positive emotions when they watch me doing the job that I love. Plus, I get standing ovations every night. What an honor!"

Before training sessions, a world champion boxer will say, "I want to become the best so that I can inspire people to believe in themselves and have ambitious dreams."

I encourage you to create your own *why*. Two tips to keep in mind. First: keep your *why* fairly short so that it's easy to remember. Second: use words that are meaningful to you.

Have to vs. want to

We often hear people say

- I *have* to go to work.
- I *have* to eat better.
- I *have* to get back into shape.

"Have to" implies an obligation to do something, like some external force pushing us to act. "Have to" is threatening. If you don't do it, there are consequences. "Have to" isn't useful for reaching your goals.

In contrast, *"want to"* has a certain power to it. Saying "I want to," comes from within, it's in our control. It's a decision that we consciously make.

When we compare the two, the differences are obvious.

For example, consider "I have to eat better" as opposed to "I want to eat better." Wanting to do something will always beat having to.

Saying "I want to" encourages us to take action, rather than put ourselves in the position of feeling forced to do something. "I want to" is much more constructive and becomes an affirmative statement. When Olympians revert back to saying "I have to go to training," I'll ask them *why*?

I have to go to training. *Why?*

To tweak my downhill position. *Why?*

To go faster down the course. *Why?*

Because I *want* to win.

Such a different perspective! So, *that's* the reason for going to training. Suddenly, they show up for training with a completely different mindset.

When we *really want* something, we're prepared to do anything to get it. Pro snowboarder Maxence Parrot is a great example. At the age of nine, he decided that he'd had enough of downhill skiing. "I want to snowboard," he told his parents. Avid downhill skiers, they didn't like the idea too much. Young Maxence, persistent fellow that he is, kept bugging his parents until they finally agreed, but on one condition: Max had to buy the snowboard himself. They thought that this would curb his enthusiasm. Who has enough money at age nine to buy their own snowboard? All it did was fuel the fire. That summer, Maxence borrowed his father's old lawnmower and mowed every lawn in the neighborhood to earn enough money to buy his first snowboard a few months later.

When you walk into the office, do you say "I *have to* work" or "I *want to* work?"

Sharing your dream

Olympians never achieve their dreams on their own; it's through teamwork that Olympic dreams come to life. Coaches, parents, and friends are well aware of the athlete's ambitious goals. By sharing our dream goals with the people around us, we take ownership of them. On the one hand, we become so much more accountable for our actions, and therefore, make a greater effort when faced with challenging moments. On the other, we'll be able to count on these people to help us reach our goals. Clearly, they won't be able to offer their support if they don't know what we're trying to accomplish.

Share what you're striving for! Your family and friends need to know your intentions if you want their help. When we're on the highway, we signal our intention to pass in the left lane. We use the blinker to *alert* others that we're changing lanes. Courteous drivers will let us pass.

If we want support, we have to ask for it; that's how elite athletes realize big dreams.

If you don't ask, you don't get!

Visualize the dream

Drawing your dream goals is a powerful way to bring them to life. Without knowing it, Mikaël Kingsbury used this strategy when he posted his drawing *I will win* over his bed. An image that we associate with our dream becomes a constant reminder of what it is that we are striving to achieve.

Last year, I helped a business leader create his own personal dream board, which led him to organizing his goals much better. He focused on three specific streams: family, work, and himself.

Remember, a picture is worth a thousand words. Drawings make us reflect, visualize, and dream. Today, the business leader

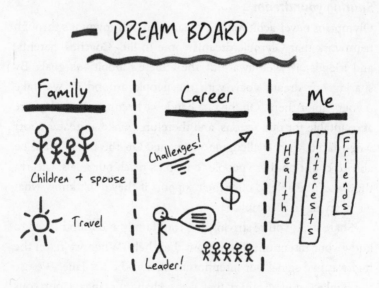

is fulfilled and happy because he accomplished a few dream goals and is excited to chase the other ones.

So, what are you waiting for? Go on and discover the ambitious Olympian in you.

Dream big!

CHAPTER 3

Feed Your Inner Fire

In March 2017, I received a phone call from a boxer who was looking for a mental performance coach. We talked about her journey, her past successes, and her needs. I googled her and discovered that she's a five-time world champion in . . . karate! Surprised, I asked her what her dream goal was, and she told me, "I want to be the first woman to become world champion in karate *and* boxing." She now had my full attention.

Her name is Marie-Ève Dicaire. Rarely have I met an athlete as strong-minded and determined as she is. In addition to having a relentless work ethic, she sets herself apart from most athletes with her energetic, charismatic, and audacious personality. During our sessions, she demands to be bombarded with information, theories, and concepts. She takes endless notes so that she can become a better student of her game. She's a dream athlete for any coach.

After we began working together, she won a string of convincing victories. Finally, in December 2018, she got her first shot at a world title, the International Boxing Federation belt, in Quebec City. In preparation, we came up with self-confidence strategies to utilize during the fight. She used them with flying colors.

I still remember our chat a few hours before her fight. We were sitting alone high up in the empty seats in the arena, which had become my office for the day.

"What are you expecting tonight?" I asked her.

She answered calmly and convincingly. "I know it's going to go well. Tonight, I'm going to be world champ."

It was said in an unpretentious and humble yet confident manner. That night, Marie-Ève made history and achieved her dream goal by becoming the first woman to become world champion in both boxing and karate.

The ultimate need: to reach the top

When we coach athletes preparing for the Olympic Games, we want them to be at their *peak*. What we mean by peak is simply being at the top of their game.

Given that the Olympic Games happen every four years — what's known as the *quad* — we consider every detail, big or small, that can allow an athlete to peak technically, physically, and psychologically at just the right time. They must be ready to be the best, to overcome the pressure, and to face unexpected challenges along the way. Each day of the quad is planned and structured to reach the top.

During this cycle, athletes compete in different competitions like world cups, grand slams, and world championships. These events act as a series of checkpoints, where coaching staff can measure the progress made from one competition to the next and tweak the yearly training plan depending on the different outcomes.

If you were to ask any coach, "What is the most important feeling to have heading into the Games?" they would probably say confidence. Not physically fit, focused or happy, but simply *confident*. As coaches, we want the athlete to believe that they have everything it takes to deliver the best performance of their life on the biggest stage.

Self-confidence is also essential in the workplace, like during a hiring interview, an important presentation, or a business meeting with potential clients. The feeling of being at the top of our game, of being *on fire*, is both exhilarating and inspiring.

> When we're overflowing with self-confidence, we tend to lean in more, leave less room for doubt, and take more risks. Sometimes, this can also lead to feeling indestructible. When we feel like this, our intention is to *perform to win*, not to avoid losing.

Have you ever said to yourself, "I'm on fire"? Do you recall experiencing this powerful feeling? For those of you who have, let's see how we can continue to feed it. For those of you who remain doubtful, let's take the plunge together and analyze how confidence works. We'll explore how to build it, keep it, and regain it if you lose it.

Self-confidence: how to find it

Over the course of my career, I've noticed that the primary reason people come to see me for personalized, one-on-one mental coaching is because of their lack of self-confidence. When we succeed in building self-confidence, we feel fantastic, but when we don't, and the doubts remain, the feeling is unbearable.

Nicolas Gill, multiple Olympic medalist and now head coach at Judo Canada, keeps reminding me as I'm working with his athletes, "If you stand on the tatami and you don't know how you can win, you've already lost the fight." He is so right.

Who wants to lead a team meeting while doubting their abilities? Who feels at ease speaking in front of an audience with butterflies in their stomach? These situations happen all the time.

- I'm writing an important exam in a month, and I don't know if I'll be ready.
- I've got an interview in a week. I'm stressed out and not sure I'll be convincing enough.
- I'm not sure if I can beat my opponent.
- I don't think I have what it takes to be a good leader.

The Olympian at work can increase their confidence just like an Olympian does for a competition. It just takes the right strategies. But where to start? How does this robust feeling work? Let's start by defining it.

Self-confidence is believing that your abilities are good enough to enable you to perform in a successful way. It's important to emphasize the word *believe* because, in the end, it's our ability to believe — or not — that will determine our level of self-confidence. I'm not alluding to spiritual beliefs, but rather the belief in our skill set.

So, how can we begin to *believe* something? There are a few fundamental principles to consider to better understand how to manage our belief system:

- It needs to fit within our value system (e.g., *doing my best* or *giving everything of myself*).
- It needs to be repeated over and over again (e.g., saying things like "I'm working hard" or "I'm giving it my all").
- It needs to be based on facts (e.g., "My boss emphasized my participation yesterday" or "A client acknowledged my expertise").

It's difficult to believe in something if it means nothing to us. Unfortunately, *believing* doesn't happen by coincidence. We build and improve our belief system through valuable lessons learned as we mature and grow. Only we can control how we gain confidence in ourselves, so it's up to us to build it properly.

The fundamental principles of self-confidence

Before we look at a few strategies to build self-confidence, let's take a few minutes to go over some fundamental principles that explain how it works. Then, implementing the strategies will be that much easier.

First, it's important to specify that self-confidence is a *feeling* and not a thought. We don't think confidence, we feel it, and feelings are never static. They evolve and move like a living thing.

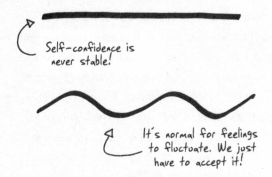

Self-confidence is never stable!

It's normal for feelings to fluctuate. We just have to accept it!

Still, what we want to avoid are the huge swings that throw us off. By understanding that our level of confidence will vary over the course of time, we can still aim to keep it at as consistent as possible.

Second, confidence is based on past experience. We gain self-confidence from tasks that we've already accomplished. We can anticipate, prepare, and get excited about the future, but we can't build any confidence by thinking about the future because it hasn't happened yet.

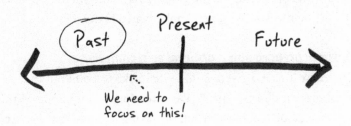

Past   Present   Future

We need to focus on this!

Third, self-confidence comes from within, not from someone else — not even your boss, your teacher, or your spouse. These people may have faith in us and believe in our skill set, but that doesn't automatically translate into self-confidence for ourselves.

For example, even if our boss were to congratulate us for a good presentation, their comments wouldn't mean much if we ourselves didn't feel that we had performed well. We'd reject the recognition. It's only our own interpretation of how we did that will have a significant impact on our confidence level. When we build a healthy dose of self-confidence, we no longer depend on the feedback of others to feel good about ourselves.

I often tell my clients, "If you feel confident, it's your fault. If you lack confidence, it's also your fault." In other words, self-confidence is something of which we are entirely in control.

Fourth, we build self-confidence from positive experiences, not negative ones. This may be stating the obvious, but we often have trouble turning the page on our less-than-successful attempts at something. We're also very good at self-criticism, right? It's so hard for us to recognize and celebrate what we've achieved. Yet humans thrive on achievement. Our brains produce feel-good hormones called endorphins when we focus on our successes. These hormonal bursts are exactly what we need to take some risks and dive right into a challenge.

The strategies to build, maintain, and regain confidence

There are numerous ways to build self-confidence, but from my work with high performers, I realized that there are five methods that are highly effective when implemented in the right way.

Optimal preparation = optimal self-confidence
Of course, this is a given. Still, I would like to point out that the word *optimal* deserves particular attention. We understand the importance of planning ahead, of having a game plan to carry

out a project or a task. Students preparing for an exam know full well the importance of studying over several days, rather than cramming until 2:00 a.m. the night before the exam. We all have memories of exams that we wrote, more or less prepared, when our confidence level was lower than usual — definitely not a great feeling! On the contrary, optimal planning would have allowed us to prepare gradually, thereby freeing us from feeling rushed or even panicked. Our state of mind would have been completely different, which makes it easier to believe in our ability to succeed.

Once we've finished preparing adequately, it's useful to stop for a few minutes and acknowledge that we've given ourselves the means to succeed. There's a sense of accomplishment that puts us into an optimal frame of mind.

For example, just before your exam, you go through your notes one last time and realize that you've successfully memorized everything. Suddenly, you become *very* sure of yourself! As you walk into the classroom, you look at the professor and think, "Bring it on!" You go from being confident to *convinced*.

The same logic applies to Olympians. They never leave anything to chance as they get ready for a competition. Optimal preparation, right down to the smallest detail, is the foundation on which their confidence rests.

- They study their opponents during video sessions.
- They talk strategy with their coaches.
- They go to bed early.
- They watch what they eat.

All this preparation is geared towards helping them show up at the starting line with the certainty that "I did what I had to do to get here. I have no regrets." Being able to say this to yourself leads to a very powerful feeling of self-belief. That's what I call optimal preparation.

During my graduate studies, I had the chance to teach a couple of courses as an associate professor. When handing out exam papers to students, I would tell them, "Good luck to those who didn't prep enough, and all the best to those who did!" For some reason, some students thought that wasn't funny.

Is your way of preparing optimal? Could you do more to increase your self-confidence before

- a meeting?
- an appointment with a client?
- the launch of a new product?
- the course you're teaching?

Just bear in mind that there's a greater risk of failing in being underprepared than there is in being overprepared.

Feeding your fire

Earlier, we referred to the expression *on fire*. We use this phrase to talk about someone who has racked up a series of good performances over time. During my time with Cirque du Soleil, I coached artists from all over the world, and they confirmed that the same expression was also used in their native languages.

Why is the expression so common? Why do we universally associate fire with a person who stands out? Why not strong like the wind or a water current, powers that are just as strong?

In my coaching, I often use a visual metaphor to make a point. For the sake of this strategy, I want you to picture a campfire. Have you ever built a campfire at the cottage, while camping, or in your backyard? Even the crackling fire on TV will do, mostly. See the burning logs and flames; hear the crackling. Blue and orange flames, bright red embers . . . it's almost hypnotic! The fire is as beautiful as it is powerful. If we don't add any logs to the fire, it will become less intense and slowly die out, right? It's predictable. (Unless it's the fire on TV!)

There's a link to be made between being on fire and the level of confidence that an Olympian feels when everything is going right for them. Their confidence level is being fed just like a blazing campfire.

To push the analogy a little further, I spoke with a friend who happens to be a firefighter. I asked him to explain the characteristics of a fire to see if I could draw other parallels between literal burning flames and an Olympian who's metaphorically on fire.

He told me that firefighters are taught to respect the *power* of a fire. We know only too well how fire can destroy homes, buildings, forests. We also say that an Olympian who's on fire commands respect. Because their successful performances over time ignite poise and strong self-belief, their opponents are well aware that they'll be *the* athlete to beat that day. Like fire, the Olympian on fire doesn't go unnoticed, another direct link to self-confidence.

My firefighter friend then pointed out that the size of the fire depends on what's feeding it. Paper, wood, or any other combustible material will increase its power, whereas water, among other things, will have the opposite effect. The same principle applies to the athlete's self-confidence. If the Olympian feeds their confidence with positive hits, it can only become more powerful. However, if they can't move beyond their mistakes, the Olympian's confidence will die like a fire doused with water. That's right, another interesting link.

Now, let's take a moment to go back to our campfire. I would argue that there are two distinct ways to feed it. First, because we're sitting comfortably in our lawn chair, glass in hand, we wait until the fire has almost gone out before adding more wood. We choose the bigger logs to avoid having to get up too frequently. But the bigger logs will take time to catch fire, and the fire may not catch the way we want it to. The end result: a big fire, then a small one, then big, then small. This method is *reactive*.

Avoid at all costs!

There is a second way that is *proactive*. I mentioned earlier that the fire will weaken and shrink over time. It's predictable. As a result, a proactive fire-feeder would stack some twigs and small logs next to their chair to feed the fire as needed. As soon as the fire starts to go down, we add more fuel so that the variations in intensity, heat, and light will be less. A savvy fire-feeder might not wait until the fire dwindles before adding fuel, they'll just keep feeding it to keep it consistent and maybe even grow it.

Much more stable!

Self-confidence works the same way. Waiting for your confidence to be sapped before reacting and feeding it is not the best strategy. You'll go through a series of ups and downs. Plus, relying solely on big victories to build self-belief isn't effective because it only happens on occasion, like putting a big log on the fire when it's low. Still, between the ups and downs are a whole bunch of smaller moments of success that deserve our attention. Arriving at a meeting well prepared, helping a colleague with a file, or executing an exercise properly in the gym . . . these small victories happen all the time. They're the kindling that keeps the fire going strong.

I refer to this technique as "acknowledging and celebrating the small wins." Or, put another way, "catching yourself being good." We're always quick to remember what we did badly, yet it's just as important to recognize and celebrate what we did well.

Spanish tennis superstar Rafael "Rafa" Nadal embodies this technique so well. If you follow professional tennis even a little, you'll have noticed that, during a game, Nadal celebrates each of his small wins in a self-assured manner. Whether it's an impressive, decisive forehand that nicks the baseline or a rally during which his opponent faults, he celebrates by shouting and pumping his fist. During a lengthy match against Roger Federer, I, with pad and pen in hand, made a note of every one of Nadal's fist pumps; I counted eighty-two of them! Nadal's cheerful celebrations boost his confidence and build momentum throughout a match. He constantly feeds his fire through small wins. Tennis fans know that Nadal sometimes starts matches slowly, but typically never runs out of gas and ends with a bang. And, like a fire, he certainly doesn't go unnoticed.

A few years ago, a professional hockey player reached out for mental training services, looking to be optimally prepared for the upcoming season. At the time, he was a ten-goal scorer and was looking to double that number.

"How do you feed your confidence?" I asked.

"By scoring goals," he immediately replied.

I told him about the fire metaphor. He was hooked. He quickly understood that relying solely on scoring was not enough. Together, we drew up a fairly long list of things that he did well:

- adequate warm-ups
- finishing a check
- napping before a game
- using mindful breathing on the bench
- listening to the coach's instructions

Through this exercise, we found twenty-five examples. He read his list regularly and made a conscious effort to acknowledge and celebrate these little wins. The following year, he scored eighteen times, just shy of the goal he had set for himself. No slumps, no big highs and lows. During the season, there were a few times when the coach told him, "You're on fire this year!" In response, the player said, "Thanks. That was the plan!" He's still feeding his fire to this day.

In the sports world, athletes celebrate their successes. It's common and accepted. Caught up in the moment, they spontaneously raise their arms, hug each other, high-five each other, do a little dance, or scream with joy. Successful moments in the workplace often occur in silence, yet it's just as important to celebrate small wins at work, such as

- handing in a well-written report,
- resolving a conflict,
- coming up with a good idea during a meeting,
- arriving at the office on time (a major win for parents with young children!); and even
- answering emails on time.

Celebrate like Rafa! Take the time to congratulate yourself. Recognize the win, even if it's just for yourself. You don't need to scream or to post it on Facebook. Highlighting it for your benefit alone — emphasizing your own, personal victory — is neither pretentious nor arrogant, it's simply an opportunity to feed your self-confidence that shouldn't be missed. Human brains are fueled by accomplishments, so take advantage of this natural mechanism. Perceiving a situation as a win releases endorphins and makes us more resistant to stressful moments.

I've shared this technique with many of my business clients, and it's always well received. So much so that some of them have decided to begin their team meetings by going around the table and asking each person to share a small victory. It creates a highly positive and pleasant atmosphere and is a great way to start any meeting. By sharing small wins with others, not only do we become accountable to keep celebrating them, we also hear our colleagues' small successes, which could be examples of achievements that we wouldn't have considered celebrating ourselves.

Let me offer a few basic principles to help you put this technique into practice:

- No victory is too small, just like a fire can feed itself off a tiny dry twig.
- Better to feed your fire often, even if you do it a little at a time, rather than a lot only once in a while.
- A series of small victories has a much stronger and lasting psychological effect than a rare, bigger win.

I have to say that this technique is my favorite because it's simple, easy to use, and so effective.

Reliving successful moments

I would like you to take a few minutes to remember a time when you delivered an exceptional performance. It can be a feat you performed recently or a long time ago. Regardless of the timeline, our emotional memory is quite powerful and can recall many details, especially when it's a positive event.

Take a few minutes to picture the situation. Where were you? Who was with you? Try to remember the setting.

Now, think about your performance. What were you doing? Relive the feelings of joy, pride, and satisfaction. It feels good, doesn't it?

Remembering a successful moment is a great confidence-boosting technique. Recalling a past performance in the present allows us to relive the same full range of emotions that we experienced when we performed the feat at the time. It makes us feel strong and offers a comforting and soothing effect. As stated previously, we build self-confidence based on the facts, on the things that we did well.

This strategy works well because we can use it anywhere, at any time. We simply need to stop and dive back into our memories for a short moment. These past performances belong to us; no one can take them away. So why not take advantage of them more often?

Canadian pro snowboarder Max Parrot competes in an event called big air. He takes off down a 150-foot-high ramp, hits the jump at speeds over forty miles per hour, executes several flips and twists while flying as high as a three-storey building, and finds a way to stomp (snowboard jargon for landing clean) his jump on a 40 percent grade landing. Please, don't try this at home! Big air jumping requires a lot of courage and self-belief.

Max is a big fan of this technique of reliving successful past performances; when competing, he does so before every jump. When he's at the top of the ramp and is just about to take off, the butterflies in his gut usually start fluttering. He plans to execute a frontside triple cork 1620, or, in layman's terms, take off forward with three back flips, making four and a half rotations while grabbing his board throughout the entire maneuver. It's easy to understand why he's stressed; he's only human!

Even though he's done this trick hundreds of times, performing this kind of jump is still dangerous. To get rid of the butterflies, he takes a moment to visualize this same jump executed perfectly during the practice session the day before. He reconnects with the moment and focuses all of his attention on the small, yet important, details:

- reaching the perfect speed on the ramp
- hitting the jump with patience and precision
- executing his acrobatic moves perfectly in the air
- connecting with his spatial awareness
- stomping the landing

Self-confidence sets in. Suddenly, he hears the official at the start gate asking him if he's ready, he nods, and drops into the course. Showtime!

Recognized for his consistency, Max is one of the best snowboarders of his generation. It's easy for him to use mental training techniques, like this one, to help him stay on top of his game.

When you use this technique, don't always pick the same successful moment. Change it up — otherwise, your moment will lose meaning and power through overuse.

You're not feeling it? Fake it!

The legendary boxer Muhammad Ali advocated that, if you want to be a champion, you need to believe that you're the best, and if you're not the best, act as if you were.

For years, positive psychology researchers insisted that our thoughts have a direct impact on our behavior and on our approach towards life in general. Basically, they suggested that when we have an optimistic mindset, our actions and, consequently, our life events are affected positively.

Recently, some researchers looked at the opposite effect, namely how our behavior influences our thoughts. Social psychologist Amy Cuddy believes that our body language has a profound impact on our level of self-confidence and the image we project. You may have already watched her TED Talk on this topic, which went viral, with more than fifty million views. In March 2018, Cuddy published a study in the scientific journal *Psychological Science* in which she explained how *power posing* allows people to feel stronger and more confident during critical moments.

What does this posture look like? The reality is, we do it instinctively. It involves keeping your

- head high,
- shoulders relaxed,
- chest out,

- face calm,
- gaze focused; and
- arms spread wide.

I tell my clients all the time to display body language that conveys poise and swagger as often as possible, even if they don't feel that way. You may be skeptical, but trust me, this technique works magic. I've seen the results and the benefits repeatedly. Sports clients will use an expansive posture during a competition to send a clear message to their opponents, warning them, "I'm ready, I'm confident, and I believe I will win."

On the other hand, if an athlete crosses their arms, slouches their shoulders, and looks down just before their turn, their opponent will quickly realize that the athlete poses no threat that day. To establish a correlation between an expansive posture and feeling powerful, Amy Cuddy mostly focused on animal behavior. For example, before a lion is about to pounce on his prey, he'll watch it closely and move with care and complete control, assume a power pose, and attack. Its prey has no hope of escaping.

This "fake-it-until-you-feel-it" technique is especially effective in combat sports, like boxing, karate, or judo, where intimidation can become a decisive factor. This confidence-booster technique is also useful in less combative sports in which athletes square off against each other, like tennis, golf, gymnastics, and track and field.

At work, persuasive body language can be an asset when you're selling a product, negotiating a contract, or holding important discussions. Provocative body language can also *attract* others. We are naturally drawn to people who appear confident, aren't we? It's fascinating to realize just how much we draw conclusions about people based on their body language.

When a colleague arrives at the office smiling, we automatically think that she's in a good mood without knowing her true frame of mind. We judge and analyze others by their appearance all the time. Did you ever realize that others, too, analyze your

body language as soon as you enter a room? The messages your posture transmits are picked up almost instantaneously. Be careful!

I've been a professional speaker for more than a decade, and I still get nervous before going up on stage. When that happens, I tell myself that the three hundred people in front of me can't know what's going on in my head, but their six hundred eyes can certainly see what my body is telling them! So, I make a conscious effort to go up on stage with a big smile on my face while displaying a convincing, expansive posture. I quickly realize that the audience is responding to what my body language is telling them. The mirror effect unfolds before my eyes: people are smiling, paying attention, and ready to hear my speech. I then feel a huge wave of self-belief wash over me. The talk starts, and I know that everything will go well.

As a baseball fan, when I think of power posing, it reminds me of the legendary pitcher Dennis Eckersley. He spent twenty-four seasons in the majors and was inducted into the Baseball Hall of Fame in 2004. Eck, as he was called, used his impressive frame, dark mane, big eyes, intimidating stare, and unorthodox pitching style to challenge batters. If you don't know who Eck is, you may want to google him. Thanks to his body language, he would win the mental battle even before he'd thrown a pitch. The message that his body was sending was something along the lines of "You'll never hit what I throw," even if at certain points in his career he certainly would have felt doubt. Even if he didn't feel confident with each pitch, he would have *looked* as if he did.

Our thoughts follow their own path

How many times has someone told you to keep your emotions in check or to relax during stressful or high-pressure moments? Probably fairly often. Our parents, bosses, coaches, colleagues, and professors regularly remind us to stay calm when things heat up. Yet, for all the times that we're told to control our emotions, how many people told you exactly how to do that? Very few, right?

So, how *do* we control our emotions exactly?

As we said at the beginning of this chapter, self-confidence is an emotion, not a thought; we *feel* confidence, we don't think confidence. We'll discuss in greater detail how emotions work in the coming chapters, but for now, it's important to remember that everything begins with a *thought*.

Thoughts lead to emotions and our brains believe what they hear, so the content of your thoughts will impact the way you feel.

Our
thoughts ———————— influence ————————▷ Our
emotions

To build and maintain self-confidence, your inner chatter needs to be constructive, optimistic, and positive. A few years back, I came up with an innovative strategy to help performers benefit from optimal self-talk. But before I explain it to you, I would like to provide some background.

Unfortunately, doping is quite common in elite sports. Some athletes compromise their health to go faster or become stronger.

Clearly, I'm against doping in sports, however, I've always been curious to better understand why athletes do it. After reading *The Secret Race* by professional cyclist Tyler Hamilton, I understood that some athletes are prepared to do anything to gain a physiological advantage.

What if we could create the same advantage, but mentally?

That's when I came up with a new mental toughness approach that I call *psychological doping*. Just like physiological doping, the moment you decide to begin doping mentally is crucial. This technique involves using additional positive and constructive self-talk during the days immediately before a competition, telling yourself good things about the upcoming event.

- "I will attack the challenge!"
- "The pressure will not get to me."
- "My plan will work!"

This will allow the athlete to feel more confident going into a competition. When used properly, this technique can generate a significant mental edge.

I encourage psychological doping at the office, too! Have a particularly constructive talk with yourself before a significant challenge.

- "I will close that deal."
- "The meeting will go my way!"
- "I will be resilient until the end."

Use positivism to dope. This perfectly natural strategy won't break any rules.

In this chapter, I defined self-confidence, how it works, and how to use it to perform better. Most of the anecdotes shared relate to sports, but you can take the same self-confidence techniques and use them in the workplace. Building, maintaining, or regaining self-confidence is much easier than most would think, wouldn't you agree? Keep in mind that the goal isn't to use all the strategies, but rather to use the strategy best suited to the moment according to your needs.

CHAPTER 4

Your Brain Is Listening

What subject did you like the least at school? Math? French? Geography? In my case, it was chemistry.

Imagine you have this class from 8:00 until 9:00 a.m. What do you say to yourself before walking into the classroom? How do you picture the next hour? "This will suck!" Did you arrive early? Unlikely. We usually show up at the last minute to things we don't enjoy. The class hasn't started yet, but you're already thinking that it will be long and boring. We're all the same. Were you more distracted? Did you look at the clock every five minutes? Under these circumstances, we're less likely to learn or get much pleasure from discovering something new. As anticipated, the class feels like it's dragging, and this subject certainly won't be our favorite. Typically, your lowest grades on your report card were from these kinds of classes.

Which subjects did you like the most? History? Drama? French? You're probably expecting me to say gym class. In fact, my favorite subject was math. Like me, you're probably less inclined to drag your feet when you walk into your favorite class. Before class starts, we're telling ourselves that it will be interesting, and we even show up a little early. We learn better, have more fun, and get higher grades.

The point I want to make is that the class itself has almost no impact on our performance. Instead, it's our attitude towards it that determines whether we'll pay attention or not.

> Our thoughts significantly influence our behavior.

I was always fascinated by my friends who would show up to chemistry class excited, full of curiosity, and ready to learn. We went to the same class, had the same teacher, and were taught the same subject matter. But the way I perceived chemistry dictated the rest. If I had adopted a different outlook, the result would have been different. For example, I could have told myself, "Okay, so it's not my favorite subject, but I'm going to make an effort to sit at the front of the class to pay closer attention, then I'm going to stop saying that the teacher is boring. I'll see how it goes." I can't say that chemistry would have suddenly become my favorite subject, or that my final grade would have jumped 20 percent, but modifying my attitude would have triggered a series of smaller, more constructive changes. Whether we like it or not, we end up building our reality based on the thoughts we have.

What does your self-talk sound like at work?

- What's your frame of mind in the morning? "Man, it's going to be a long day today" or "My busy day will go well. One step at a time."
- How do you prepare for a meeting with your boss? "I don't like him!" or "Focus on the importance of the meeting, and things will be better."
- What message is your inner chatter sending to your brain before a presentation? "I'm not going to be

good enough this morning" or "I know my stuff. I'll be great."

Be careful because your brain hears everything you say, even if you don't say it out loud.

See both sides of the coin

The performers I coach live in all sorts of situations, some more complex than others. Sometimes, my job is to challenge them to look in a different way at the situation that's bothering them. In other words, to help them see the other side of the coin.

An Olympian once said to me, "If I blow it at the Games, I'll be letting down thirty-six million Canadians." Not all Canadians follow the Olympic Games, but I understood his viewpoint. It's *one* way of seeing things. So, I encouraged him to look at it from another angle. I'm fully aware that the thought of letting people down is a very powerful, scary feeling and, as such, it carries real weight. From the start, when the athlete is deeply rooted in the negative emotion, it's extremely difficult to look at a situation from another point of view. I love having these conversations. We explore options together until the original thought has faded just enough to allow other perspectives to emerge. These conversations can be difficult and heavy at times because of the strong emotions involved.

In this case, we came up with something like, "If I perform the way that I prepared, my country will be proud of me. Results aren't everything." Now, that's much better.

I never blame the athlete for their initial thought. The sole purpose of the exercise is to help the Olympian understand that their self-talk can either limit or help them. It's a choice.

Many clients have told me that when they face a problematic situation, they now ask themselves, "How would JF challenge me to look at this scenario?" I prefer being the little angel, not the devil, on their shoulder!

> When we change the way we look at things,
> the things we look at *change*.

We're creatures of habit. The thoughts we have about a situation that we experience over and over again rarely change. A psychology professor told me that 95 percent of the thoughts of people who experience routine day-to-day activities are more or less the same from one day to the next. Scary, isn't it? Basically, once we've decided to look at a situation in a certain way, we rarely think of questioning it.

For example, consider the FedEx logo. It's a sign that you've seen again and again. When you look at it, you probably see the letters F-e-d-E-x. What if I were to say to you that you could also see something else? Look at the space between the E and the x. You'll see an arrow pointing to the right.

Ever since someone pointed this out to me, I always see the arrow first. This logo proves that we end up seeing what we're looking for.

How many times do you look at a situation in the same way? Are some of your thoughts limiting the way you perceive things without you realizing it?

Just as a coin has two sides, there's always another way to see any situation.

Enough with the catastrophic thinking!

In the course of my career, I've worked with people representing more than forty different nationalities. Over time, I noticed certain cultural differences in the way people perceived the same reality.

As a proud Canuck, I am happy to say that Canadians are some of the most open, nice, welcoming, hard-working, and fun-loving people. However, I've also noticed that Canadians tend to exaggerate and dramatize events. Complaining and whining are popular pastimes. For instance, some of us feel sorry for ourselves as winter approaches because we can't accept the reality of colder weather coming our way, as if winter wasn't supposed to show up this year! We don't accept the situation and end up working against it instead of *with* it.

> The act of *complaining* is like rocking back and forth in a comfortable chair. It offers temporary comfort, but it doesn't get you anywhere!

The tendency to dramatize often occurs during the most stressful moments. We quickly jump to conclusions and become impulsive and reactive.

For example, let's take a hockey player who makes a mistake. He causes a giveaway that leads to an opposing goal. The coach calls the player back to the bench and . . . boom! Wild thoughts begin to race through his mind:

- "Why'd I do that?"
- "Bye-bye, ice time!"
- "Well, no more power-play shifts for me."
- "I'm such a loser."
- "I'll never get drafted."

These catastrophic thoughts take no more than a few seconds to go from "Why'd I do that?" to "I'll never get drafted."

We know, logically, that the mistake wasn't all that important. But in a situation in which we're under pressure, catastrophic thoughts have free rein because we're in a vulnerable state. The problem isn't that we made a mistake; everyone makes mistakes. The real issue is the way we perceive our mistake.

The hockey player should, instead, be aware of the risk of spiralling out of control if he lets his disastrous thinking overwhelm him. Allowing this thought pattern to happen only deepens his anxiety and the negativism. Being self-critical isn't a problem per se, as reflecting back on what happened leads to finding solutions. But we'll come back to this a little later.

This hockey player needs to interrupt the illogical sequence of disastrous thoughts that end up being completely detached from reality. "Whoa, I'm digging myself into a hole. That's enough. Back to reality." The inner chatter must be reset to get back to helpful thinking.

By simply breaking the sequence of negative thinking, we can redirect ourselves and reach a calmer state of mind in a matter of seconds, as shown in the following diagram. Choosing path y over path x yields a significantly different outcome.

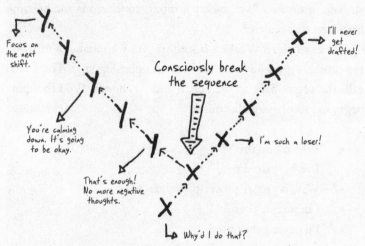

In the end, it isn't the problem that is the problem. The real problem is your attitude toward the problem!

Be aware

Below is an exercise that I use during mental coaching sessions to show the impact that our attitude can have on a situation. There are two scenarios:

> Scenario A: You just had a *tough* day at work. You feel that the meetings you attended weren't very effective, you couldn't stay focused, and you made a few dumb mistakes. About 60 percent of your day was bad.
>
> Scenario B: You just had a *great* day. You felt productive, focused, and confident. You feel that you dealt with a lot of work effectively. You were on fire and rate your day as 90 percent successful.

Let's analyze these two scenarios from two different angles: a *negative/pessimistic/destructive* mindset and a *positive/optimistic/constructive* mindset.

Let's consider Scenario A (tough day) through the *negative/pessimistic/destructive* lens. It's no surprise that you're focused on the bad things that happened during the day. You tell yourself that your bad day unfolded as expected. You dramatize the consequences of your mistakes and find excuses to explain the bad day. You see yourself as a victim, put yourself down, and decide that tomorrow won't be any better. This sequence of negative thoughts can make you fearful, anxious, and highly uncertain about the future.

On the flip side, how would you see the *tough* day if you used a *positive/optimistic/constructive* attitude? You would try to counterbalance it by focusing on what you did well, even if this represents no more than 40 percent of your day. You would draw lessons from the things that didn't go so well. The poorly executed tasks cannot be excused; they would become useful information to help you bounce back quickly. You would take responsibility for the situation without putting yourself down. You would see this as a one-off situation and say to yourself that things will be better the next day.

A tough day at the office

ATTITUDE Negative/Pessimistic/Destructive	ATTITUDE Positive/Optimistic/Constructive
– focus on mistakes – the bad day was expected – find excuses – feel like a victim – become anxious	– identify the 40% – learn from the experience – take responsibility – look forward to bouncing back – things will be better tomorrow

Now, let's consider Scenario B, having a *great* day, through the *negative/pessimistic/destructive* lens. You don't believe that you're the reason behind your own success. "I was lucky!" You see this great day as being the exception, not the rule. Typically, you'll acknowledge that it was a good day, *but* . . . "Yes, it was a good performance, *but* I missed the shot, *but* I got a penalty, *but* the opposing team scored when I was on the ice." When you use "yes, but. . ." you only emphasize the words that follow *but*, whether it's a mistake, a fault, or a tiny slip-up. You discard everything that comes before *yes*. It's much better to use *"yes . . . and . . ."* to recognize what also precedes the word *and*, which typically refers to what went right. In the end, it's a missed opportunity to build self-confidence thanks to all the small wins earned during the day.

Choosing to see the situation with a *positive/optimistic/constructive* mindset is very different. You're able to acknowledge and congratulate yourself for the small victories. You go over what made your day so great to be able to reproduce it in the future. As for the 10 percent that didn't go well, you take it with a grain of salt while still noting the opportunities to learn and improve.

A great day at the office

ATTITUDE	ATTITUDE
Negative/Pessimistic/Destructive	Positive/Optimistic/Constructive
– this great day was a lucky break	– proud of the good things
– it was a good day, BUT . . .	– want to reproduce this good day
– emphasize the 10%	– 10% → an opportunity to learn
– missed opportunity to build self-confidence	– Confidence booster for the future

You may not be an extreme pessimist or optimist, but you're certainly somewhere on the spectrum between the two.

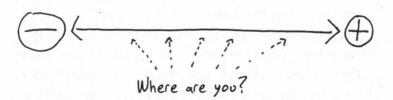

Where are you?

Through which lens do you feel you view your life? Are you influenced more by one or the other? Do stressful moments affect your attitude? Do you tend to switch lenses based on who you're with?

In the end, no matter what kind of day you're having, only you can turn it into a learning experience. The lens you choose will color how you perceive your reality.

Do I always need to be positive?

Positive psychology first appeared in 1998. It was the dawn of the new millennium, and modern psychology was changing along with the times. Since then, multiple books have been published on this topic, not least of which are those by Dr. Martin Seligman, who is considered the father of positive psychology. He's published more than 250 scientific articles and twenty books, most of them bestsellers that have been translated into more than twenty languages.

Why has positive psychology suddenly become so popular?

There's a desperate need. We live in a world of international disputes, terrorist attacks, climate change, global pandemics, social injustice, collusion, fake news, hate messages, manipulation, and harmful working conditions. Beautiful and desirable things are trafficked all over social media, manipulating us, whether or not we want to be. We feel envious when we look at our friends' ten vacation snapshots of a tropical paradise, *#bestvacationever*. Is that real life? Is the grass really greener on the other side? When we compare, many of us end up thinking that our lives are pretty awful. Under these circumstances, it's easy to see why books on positive psychology have gained so much traction.

Of course, having a positive attitude isn't *the* miracle cure for a world of negativism. Being a "cheerleader" doesn't protect us from feeling miserable, since reality is much more complicated than that. When I coach my clients, I make sure they understand that there's a difference between having a positive attitude and having the *right* attitude.

Imagine that you have a twelve-hour workday ahead of you, filled with meetings and ongoing projects. At four in the afternoon, you feel tired and need a jolt, but you have to work until seven. You want to persevere, so you choose the right attitude and say to yourself, "I'm going to focus on the next task and forget about the rest for now. I'll make it. I've done a lot more compared to what's left." This self-talk is constructive, supportive, and practical.

Here's another example. You made every effort to deliver a report on time. Your boss reads it and suddenly you find yourself at the receiving end of a tongue-lashing: "This file is not to our standards!" Your boss decides that you've spent enough time on it and that the project will never see the light of day. Under these circumstances, would the right attitude be to say, "That's okay. It's not the end of the world. There'll be other projects"?

No way. The feelings of frustration and anger, justified under the circumstances, would be suppressed, denied, and swept under the rug. The right attitude here is to acknowledge the disappointment and process the criticism of having underperformed.

I recall some Olympian clients who were angry because they had underperformed but were able to move on, in contrast to many of their rivals. Sure, they criticize themselves, but not for long. Great champions have this ability to avoid getting bogged down in catastrophic thinking and quickly regain a constructive attitude.

Taking the time to cushion the blow isn't negative in itself; emotions must be expressed. They also reflect a deep desire to succeed.

Georges St-Pierre, aka GSP, learned this the hard way. He's recognized as one of the best mixed martial artists to ever step into the octagon. During his fifteen-year professional career, he successfully defended the UFC welterweight title nine times while putting up an overall record of twenty-six wins and two losses.

A few years ago, I heard GSP speak at a leadership event, and one anecdote he shared really caught my attention.

On April 7, 2007, GSP was the favorite to win against American Matt "The Terror" Serra to defend his title for the first time. He thought the win would come easy, but to his surprise, the fight turned out to be a bitter lesson in humility. He performed poorly and lost badly. Embarrassed and humiliated, GSP vowed to do everything he could from that moment on to avoid feeling these unpleasant emotions ever again. He chose to make several changes to his training regimen, and they worked. He used this devastating loss as motivation to get better and stronger than ever. GSP retired twelve years later, unbeaten since his heartbreaking fight against the Terror.

His negative experience led to a positive one.

Contrasts can help

I've noticed in my coaching that we learn a lot from *contrasts*. We savor successful moments more after experiencing a few failures. In the same way, we enjoy good times after having experienced setbacks and adversity. We realize how important our health is after we've been sick. We appreciate the summer because we froze all winter. Cubans don't appreciate warm weather like we Canadians do because they have it year-round!

As we saw in GSP's story, both positive and negative experiences offer opportunities to learn. The experiential contrasts force us to reflect, to weigh the pros and cons, and to make better choices for the future.

In our everyday lives, we spontaneously use the words positive and negative a lot to describe someone's attitude. For example, "She has a positive attitude," or "He's so negative!" Limiting ourselves to these two adjectives can oversimplify a point of view. I challenge my clients to use more specific words, to better describe mindsets.

- A *constructive* or a *destructive* attitude: will my way of thinking build or destroy my relationship with my colleague?
- *Solution-based* or *problem-based* thinking: will my strategy solve the problem or make it worse?

- A *helping* or a *harmful* attitude: will my inner chatter help me or hurt me before I begin this difficult discussion?
- An attitude that *propels* or *holds back*: will my constant self-criticism generate or limit new ideas?
- A *winning* or a *losing* attitude: will I come out of this interview having won or lost?

Finding a variety of words helps us understand our mindsets more accurately, thus elevating our thinking beyond simply contrasting positive and negative.

Clearly, the point here isn't just to be positive, but rather to choose the *right attitude*. The attitude that will best help you handle a situation correctly and make you learn some important lessons whether the conditions are good or bad.

What does it mean to be *mentally tough*?

Over time, the expression *mental toughness* has become a part of popular culture. I've coached many people throughout the years who I would consider tough mentally: Olympians, of course, but also surgeons, soldiers, actors, musicians, and corporate leaders.

> Being mentally tough means choosing the right attitude even when a situation defies you.

It's easy to have the right attitude when everything is going well. It just happens naturally. But having the right attitude when things aren't going as planned, that requires mental toughness! When an athlete won't give up despite things going badly, we hear commentators say that they are gritty, tenacious, and relentless. That's exactly what I'm talking about.

When I was starting out as a mental coach, I prepared a teen-ager for the year's most important track and field meet. The weather conditions weren't great: cold, rainy, and windy. Most of the competitors never stopped complaining. "This blows! This really sucks!" Tough as nails, the young athlete saw the situation differently.

He had packed the necessary clothing in his bag to withstand the cold. *Check.* As for the rain, he knew it wasn't going to slow him down because the Weather Network forecast wet conditions during the qualifiers, but only clouds for the final. *Check.*

"No stress," he said.

"And the wind?" I asked.

He told me that he had reached out to the organizers the night before to find out which direction he would be running in. "I'll have the wind at my back. I think I'm going to beat my personal best today!" he said. *Check.*

He had chosen the *right attitude* and ended up clocking a personal best time.

A muscular brain

Developing mental toughness is like building muscle strength. To strengthen a muscle, we train it by increasing the weight, the resistance, and the number of repetitions. The same goes for our brains. Our mental strength increases when we decide to face up to the challenges that take us out of our comfort zones. The more we train ourselves to choose the right attitude at difficult moments, the tougher and more resilient we become in the face of adversity.

Through purposeful mental training, our mind can deal with even more complex situations like muscles that can handle heavier loads. It can get to a point where some situations that flustered us in the past will seem insignificant in hindsight.

Remember the clown in Chapter 1? When it was time to pick

spectators in the audience to come up on the stage, he deliberately chose those who seemed reluctant. At each show, he intentionally challenged himself to sharpen his skills, which was his way to avoid getting stuck in a rut and to progress as an artist. He knew how to train his brain.

I would like to share a personal story. As a teenager, I was a rather shy adolescent who often lacked self-confidence when it came to tougher challenges. Sometimes, I had a bad habit of throwing in the towel before I had even tried to tackle the challenge. I preferred the easy route and was often a sore loser. (I still am, but I experience it way differently!) As a child, my parents would let me win at board games to avoid having to deal with my fits. When I tell this story to the people who know me today, they have a hard time imagining JF acting that way.

I remember avoiding situations that made me feel vulnerable. Being a perfectionist, I didn't want to risk failing and looking bad in front of others. It was only when I attended university that I realized that I had a lot to gain by changing my impeding attitude. So I decided to attack my weaknesses, and by weaknesses I mean the fear of speaking in public, the need to dodge sensitive discussions, and the intense dislike for being criticized.

I admit it, at the time I was mentally weak.

I rarely chose the right attitude in tough situations. I was more inclined to find excuses to explain my mistakes and to run away from moments of vulnerability. Luckily, some professors at university saw greater potential in me. Through them, I understood that I was limiting my personal growth because of my disruptive perfectionist mindset.

Thanks to their advice and the performance psychology training, I was able to look at things from another angle. I began to willingly put myself in situations that pushed my limits. I tamed the discomfort of feeling vulnerable. Little by little, I set goals that were bold. In the end, I succeeded in breaking free, and I say *break free* because I really felt imprisoned by my former mindset.

I was the shy JF; now I'm a sought-after speaker. I was the JF who avoided sensitive topics; I now have fierce conversations with clients every day. I was the JF who hated criticism; I now ask clients to provide honest feedback about my work. I feel that I've transitioned from being mentally weak to being mentally tough. I'm proud of the changes I've made, and I now get to coach people in the same direction.

Essentially, all we can do is embrace the challenges and choose the right attitude.

Everything starts between the ears

While working on new acrobatic tricks, one of the Cirque du Soleil trapeze artists would say, "I'm always one thought away from doing it right." He was right. A single thought can change our performance. The right thought can lead to an exceptional performance, while negative inner chatter can lead to failure.

- I won't be able to do it.
- I won't be at my best.
- They won't like me.
- It won't be as good as the last time.

Do you have these kinds of thoughts? Do you recognize them in someone you know?

Everything starts between the ears. It's like the electrical panel in our homes. The wiring carries electricity to the power outlets, appliances, and light fixtures throughout the house. In the case of humans, the panel is our brain. The brain sends orders through the nervous system to the different body parts to do what's needed to perform.

Let's look at the following image to explain the impact of inner chatter on our behavior. There are three aspects to performance: psychological, emotional, and physical.

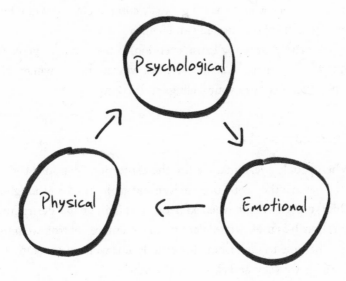

The psychological aspect refers to what we think (our thoughts), the emotional aspect represents what we feel (our emotions), and the physical aspect is what we do (our behaviors).

The psychological sphere is placed at the top, since everything stems from it. The thoughts we choose every day build our reality. These thoughts will have a direct impact on our emotions, while our emotions will influence our behaviors, which, in turn, will affect our thoughts. For better or for worse, it's a never-ending, self-conditioning cycle.

For example, if you feel panicky because you're about to speak to a large audience, ask yourself how you perceive the situation. If your inner chatter sounds like this, "Everyone is looking at me. If I say something wrong, they'll judge me," the nervousness will produce cortisol, the human stress hormone. Your body will tense up, your voice will rise, and your speech will accelerate. In this state, you could lose your train of thought or, even worse, draw a blank during your speech. On the other hand, if your thoughts are a little more constructive, such as, "I will take my time and speak slowly and clearly. Things will be fine," the nervousness won't go away completely, but you'll feel more in control emotionally and behaviorally.

Ultimately, bringing extra attention to the way you perceive situations can increase self-awareness, which, in turn, will enable you to better control your feelings and actions.

Figure out your brain

When people overthink, we use the expression "get out of your head" so that they don't overanalyze and get lost in their thoughts. This is especially true when someone is caught up in a destructive spiral, such as useless speculation. To gain more control, we must take the time to understand how our brains work to generate the thoughts we want and eliminate the others.

> We can't change a behavior if we don't understand what triggered it.

Think of the triple bubble diagram in the previous section. The first letter of each component — Psychological, Emotional, and Physical — spells *pep*, as in the pep talk a coach might use to get their team hyped up for a game.

Too much importance is given to pep talks. These speeches are sometimes useful, other times not at all. If an athlete counts on their coach's pep talk to get revved up for the game, they're relying on an extrinsic source for motivation, something which is out of their control. This could be dangerous because if the coach's pep talk isn't bang on, it could do the opposite and demotivate or confuse the athletes. Similarly, a worker may rely on their boss's speech, but, as we know, not all bosses have what it takes to motivate their employees.

How often are traditional pep talks useful? Do they really get you going? Is a "rah-rah" cheerleading approach what you really need?

The best pep talk, in my opinion, is the one we give ourselves. Only we know exactly what gets us going, and only we understand what message we need to hear to trigger the right emotions. Nobody understands our brains better than we do. Plus, we have full control of our inner chatter.

The only relationship that lasts forever is the one we have with ourselves. We are the person we talk to the most! All other relationships, as satisfying as they may be, are temporary. So it's critical that we get along with ourselves. We need to become our own best coach.

I encourage you to come up with your own best pep talks, like an Olympian!

The brain believes what it hears

Have you ever embellished an anecdote a little to make it more interesting and thought-provoking? You know, the type of "augmented reality" story we tell our friends after work on a Friday while having a cold, refreshing beverage. Yes? Well, you're not the only one!

"Hey! I bumped into the Toronto Raptors coach at the airport this week. We chatted about the team's success for at least five minutes. He's a great guy."

But the real version would go something more like this: "Hey! I crossed paths with the Toronto Raptors coach at the airport this week. I shook his hand and wished him good luck."

When we tell the exaggerated version the first time, we make sure that we mention the little embellishments correctly. We want to captivate our listeners' attention while making sure the story is credible. It's a little easier to tell the anecdote the second time, but not as easy as the tenth time. Sharing the story repeatedly makes the embellished version sound true. We start believing our own lie!

Comedians are the best at doing this. Most of their stories are inspired by facts, but they spice them up to entertain the crowd. To make the stories believable, they rehearse them many times over before telling them to an audience. Their storytelling abilities are so good that they make something fabricated sound real.

Why do we believe our own exaggerated stories?

For two reasons. First, because of the influential details we add to the story, and second, because of the multiple repetitions. Many of us do this constantly in our daily lives without even being conscious of it.

For example, you may say, "Nothing is going according to plan." Is this entirely true? Probably not. Some things may not be going as planned, but *everything*? Isn't this a little overdramatic?

"I'm such a loser. I can't do anything right." Really? Can anyone truly say that they fail at everything, all the time? Definitely not.

"My boss said that I am hurting the business." In fact, the boss was expecting more leadership within the department. These are two very different messages.

I could go on and on.

A problem arises when we repeatedly tell ourselves these same kinds of twisted statements, not just once or twice. Our brains are listening to our distorted story, repeated over and over again. Your mind believes your story just like your friend believed your anecdote about running into the Raptors coach at the airport.

> The brain doesn't really distinguish between what's real and what's imagined. It simply believes what it hears, not what's true.

Pay particular attention to your inner chatter. By doing so, you'll increasingly notice the link between your thoughts and your emotions. The brain is always listening. What you tell yourself repeatedly will influence the rest. It's up to you.

The benefits of having the right attitude

We hear parents, teachers, sports coaches, and bosses say how important it is to have the right attitude. Well, we should listen to them because there are important benefits to developing the right attitude. Let's explore some of these benefits — without exaggerating or twisting the examples, of course!

Laughing and smiling make us feel good

It's no secret that we face an endless number of stressful situations in our lives, such as challenges at work, family issues, gloomy international news, climate change, and more. Within this social noise, having some ways to deal with the struggles of everyday life is essential. As simple as they may seem, smiling and laughing are powerful antidotes to tougher times. We tend to forget it, but they are anti-stressors that we can use as much as we want, whenever we want.

People who have a great attitude are inclined to smile and laugh naturally. I would even say that these natural mechanisms are directly linked to maintaining the right attitude. If you have pessimistic tendencies, try to smile and laugh more often. You'll soon notice the benefits.

Below are the advantages that smiling and laughing bring:

- The body produces endorphins, the feel-good hormones. Think about how you feel after a big belly laugh.
- Laughing provides additional oxygen that spreads

quickly throughout the body and the brain and relaxes the nervous system.

- Laughing is a great workout! The diaphragm expels air from our lungs at speeds over sixty miles per hour, which increases blood flow and reduces arterial pressure.
- When we smile, several tiny facial muscles contract in a specific sequence. This sends positive messages to our brains that "Things are good!" which, in turn, contribute to a sense of well-being.
- Smiling and laughing are contagious. They foster positive relationships within a group. How can we resist smiling back when a baby smiles at us, right? We respond spontaneously to a smile.

If you can't make yourself laugh enough, you can join a laughing group. In 1995, Dr. Madan Kataria founded workshops in which people go through a series of voluntary laughing exercises. The workshops are based on the belief that voluntary laughter boasts similar physical and mental benefits as real, spontaneous laughter. This practice is commonly used to help people deal with depression and other mental illnesses. Given its effectiveness, it instantly went viral! There are now laughing clubs in every major city in the world. Curious about this practice, I enrolled in a few workshops; I loved it so much that I went through the training to become an instructor.

Did you know that children laugh approximately six times more than adults do in a day? As we age, we tend to take life too seriously and end up laughing less and less. Isn't that sad?

When I'm standing next to athletes dealing with high-pressure moments, I make a conscious effort to show a positive attitude. I'll subtly crack a smile at strategic moments to create a more relaxed atmosphere.

World champion boxer Marie-Ève Dicaire is a pro at using this strategy. Her joyous attitude and ear-to-ear smile helps her stay relaxed. Whether she's three days or three minutes away from fight time, the smile is there. Did her signature smile help her win that world title? Hard to say, but one thing's for sure: that smile puts her in an ideal frame of mind.

A few years back, I traveled for the first time with an athlete to a Grand Slam event in Europe. At the competition venue, I noticed that the funny and sarcastic person I knew during our sessions in my office had changed to a serious and cold individual. I knew him well enough to understand that this behavior was due to unnecessary self-imposed pressure.

During his warm-up, I asked him to show me his teeth. He understood that he hadn't smiled all day. He suddenly burst out laughing! Naturally, he relaxed, and ended up competing very well.

Sometimes, the best way to deal with adversity is to just *laugh it off*.

As the old saying goes, don't take life too seriously, as nobody gets out alive anyway!

Become a go-getter

The person who maintains a great working attitude will be better equipped to persevere in the face of adversity. They tend to dive in more and overcome obstacles more easily. When they get knocked down, they get up quickly and find the courage to come back stronger. Bouncing back from failure is considered a *win*. This mentality feeds the ego and reinforces the determination to push even further.

I will always remember a young gymnast who had auditioned for Cirque du Soleil. On paper, her acrobatic skill level was much lower than that of the other candidates auditioning for the same position. But this young woman never saw them as a threat. Instead, she kept her eyes on the prize and never wavered. "One day I will be a Cirque du Soleil artist," she told me. She struggled with some of the tough acrobatic and artistic training, which caused her to cry on multiple occasions. But she never gave up.

Her tears were nothing more than a way to release her emotions. She saw this challenging audition as a way to build character, which would serve as a solid foundation for her future career.

During the audition, she kept progressing, slowly but surely, thanks to her go-getter attitude. A few months later, she earned a well-deserved contract to join the legendary show *Saltimbanco*.

Fast-forward two years, and she'd become one of the best artists in the show and one of the most appreciated by her peers. The casting department who recruited her for the audition were stunned by her progress. I wasn't. The go-getter attitude makes it possible to achieve great things and sometimes reach unsuspected levels of excellence.

What type of glasses are you wearing?
Having the right attitude makes it easier to push through barriers. Athletes with great mindsets can see beyond obstacles to stay focused on reaching their goals.

Our reality is constructed from how we perceive things. Everything depends on the type of glasses we're wearing, and how they color what we see. Take a look at the following diagram.

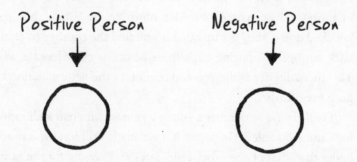

So, let's say that the circle on the left represents the positive person, and the one on the right, the negative person. As you can see, the two circles are the same diameter. Now, look at the black circles in the next drawing. Imagine that they represent distractions that could prevent someone from succeeding, such as added pressure and tough challenges.

The negative person tends to exaggerate difficult situations, to see them as bigger than they really are, which explains why the circles on the right are larger.

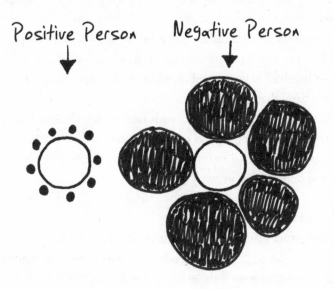

Positive Person   Negative Person

This individual is surrounded by large, self-imposed black circles that are difficult to manage. Under these circumstances, it's hard to focus on anything other than the cumbersome problems that block the light at the end of the tunnel. Discouragement isn't far away.

Now, let's look at the circle on the left. The positive person also has their share of obstacles, *but* they assign far less importance to them. They choose to see the impediments as they are. The optimist recognizes the black circles yet sees them as situations they can resolve and overcome. They don't let the distractions take over, no matter how many there are.

Look at the two white circles. Do they still appear identical? The one to the left seems bigger, doesn't it?

A hockey goalie I work with says he feels bigger when he has the right attitude. "I take up more space in the net. I cover the angles so much better." On the other hand, when his inner chatter is negative, he feels smaller and lost in his net.

One of my clients is the president of a big company in Montreal. He's an eternal optimist and an impressive problem-solver. During one session, we were chatting about his current situation at work, and I asked him if he saw the glass half empty or half full. His answer caught me by surprise. "JF, my glass is always full — one half is water, and the other half is air." Such a typical answer from that guy!

Let's finish off this section with one of my all-time favorite quotes from former British prime minister Winston Churchill: "The pessimist sees difficulty in every opportunity. The optimist sees the opportunity in every difficulty."

Take out the negative!

Our minds are programmed to think in the simplest way possible. They respond well to commands and affirmations, but not to negative words because those cloud the message. For example, if you tell your brain not to think about failure, it's baffling because the brain gets confused with sentences containing negative words. But if you tell it to think about succeeding, it understands perfectly.

> We must tell our brains *what we want*,
> not what we don't want.

Take a grocery list, for example. You write down what you want to buy. When you enter the grocery store, you head for the items on your list, even if you have hundreds of other items in front of your eyes. You're an efficient shopper. But what if you were to write things on your list that you don't need, such as "don't buy yogurt, flour, and juice." Unthinkable, right? And these would probably be the first items that catch your eye as you go up and down the aisles, even if you don't need them.

Words such as "not" or "don't" indicate what we want to avoid, which becomes a non-linear way to deliver a message to our brain. We typically use negative wording during stressful moments, when we must make a quick decision, leaving the brain no time to understand the meaning of the message. For example, in the middle of a bout, a boxer knows that they have to keep their guard up. Their message would be more effective if they were to think "Keep your hands up" as opposed to "Don't lower your hands."

There are two reasons for this.

First, when things are happening quickly, the brain is trying to pick up information as quickly as possible. It will only pay attention to the most important words, such as "lower" and "hands." The message received is, in fact, the opposite of what is desired.

Second, the brain will have to analyze the message twice to get the correct meaning. "You're asking me not to lower my hands. Therefore, you want me to keep them up." Then, *bong!* You get your bell rung with a left hook.

You've probably written a multiple-choice exam at some point in your life. Have you ever noticed how questions full of negative words are much harder to understand? Try this.

Which countries are *not* European? Choose the best answer.

a) Canada, Australia, and Argentina
b) France, Italy, and Switzerland
c) Japan, the United States, and Peru
d) Spain, Portugal, and Austria
e) a and b, but not c
f) a and c, but not d
g) a, c and f

The answer is g. Did you have to read the question and the answers a few times to understand? So confusing, right?

I took a wellness class at university that was supposed to be a walk in the park. Most of the students were doing very well heading into the midterm exam, so no one was worried. Well, as it turned out, the multiple-choice questions were full of negative words. The class average was a "brilliant" 64 percent. A few of us complained that the midterm wasn't written properly, and fortunately, the professor wrote the final exam differently. The average mark for that test was 84 percent.

Imagine your golfing partner saying, "*Don't* hit the ball into the bushes!" or your work colleague telling you as you're about to give your presentation, "Did you know that the big boss is here? No big deal, just *don't* screw up!" Not exactly what you want to hear just before an important performance.

Limit the negative words and get straight to the point.

Reduce anxiety

A pessimistic attitude can generate anxiety. When stuck in this mindset, we spend a lot of time and energy thinking about what could frighten us, harm us, or possibly threaten us. However, fear isn't an emotion that should be completely eliminated, as it can sometimes help us identify a risk and adjust to it. Yet when we let fear hold us back, it becomes a hindrance. Too much anxiety can become overwhelming.

Each time you see the negative side of a situation, it's like adding a drop of water to a glass. At some point that glass starts to fill up and get heavier. When a pessimist finds a way to look at reality a bit more optimistically, they typically feel relieved and lighter — there is less weighing down their glass.

Furthermore, if you held a glass of water with a straight arm, the glass would feel light, right? But if you hold it for several minutes, the same glass begins to feel so much heavier. The same applies with anxious thoughts that weigh on us.

Just let go!

An optimistic attitude leads to thoughts that make us feel good, happy, and calm. Do you remember the skill of celebrating small wins in Chapter 3? It's an excellent way to reinforce your positive attitude. Below are a few examples:

- Think about the good things you did during the day.
- Think about the things you are thankful for.
- Think about future projects that excite you.
- Remember the times you were happy.

Just thinking about these small wins will put you in a good mood.

When I played squash competitively, my coach was seventy years old but didn't look a day over forty-five. He had played professionally in England, so when he picked up a racket for a game, watch out! Beyond his impeccable coaching skills, it was his outlook on life that made him exceptional. "If we're so good at creating our own misery, we can be just as good at creating our own happiness," he would say. It's a choice.

Often, we let our frame of mind as soon as we wake up in the morning have a serious impact — whether good or bad — on our whole day.

- "I didn't really sleep well. It's going to be a long day at the office."
- "It's a big day at school today. At least we're starting something new. I find that really motivating."
- "We're launching our new product on the market today. I'm a little nervous, but it's an exciting moment. I'm proud of what I accomplished."

"Did you get up on the wrong side of the bed this morning?" This popular expression refers to someone who is in a bad mood. Someone chooses to be in a bad mood; it doesn't happen on its own.

On what side of the bed do you usually get up? Pay attention to your inner chatter when you start your day. Most elite athletes start their day with positive affirmations. Try it. It will brighten your day!

Caution, it's contagious!

We mentioned that smiling and laughing exude contagious positive energy. The same applies to negative energy. Who likes to be around people who are always negative? Their bad aura affects our morale and saps our energy. Did you ever notice how the atmosphere starts to quickly deteriorate when someone negative joins a group of fun and lively people? If you've played team sports, you may remember the *bad apples* on your team. I've noticed that the negative experiences in our lives affect us more than positive experiences do. This principle is called *negativity bias*. No wonder we have to put a little more effort into keeping our thoughts positive.

After my early-morning workouts at the gym, I spend a good fifteen minutes in the sauna to relax, unwind, and self-reflect. As a matter of fact, a lot of content in this book stemmed from ideas that came to me in the sauna!

From time to time, a sixty-year-old man uses the sauna while I'm there. I've never heard him say anything positive. He's a first-class grouch who's always negative. He refuses to be responsible for anything that happens to him and constantly blames others for his misfortunes. I purposefully close my eyes when he walks in so that he doesn't talk to me. Pessimism is contagious just like the flu, so I stay away!

Now, think of people who are positive. They attract other people, right? We appreciate their presence and are drawn to them because of their good mood.

Let's put this to the test. At work, you need to recruit a new member for your team, and you're pressed for time. In desperation, someone shows you photos of the following three candidates. Quickly: which one would you choose?

When I do this experiment during my talks, almost every participant chooses the image on the right. I ask them why. They tell me that this candidate seems to be

- nice,
- a good work colleague,
- happy,
- intelligent; and
- professional.

I imagine that many of you chose the same person for similar reasons. The photos show three very different types of body language. The choice is easy, yet, after only a few seconds, we're ready to welcome this individual to our team without knowing anything more about their professional career. Just a quick glance is enough to say that they would be an asset, just as the body language of candidates one and two convinced us of the opposite.

We must bear in mind that we, too, are being judged every time we walk into a room. People will draw conclusions about us, whether they're right or wrong, based on what we project physically. Whether it's when we attend a meeting, are on a first date, or are getting home after work, our body language speaks volumes without us realizing the impact it can have.

When I played junior hockey, something happened during a playoff game that still haunts me to this day. We were comfortably ahead by two goals when the other team managed to tie the game before the end of the second period. We felt the momentum suddenly switch. In the dressing room between the second and third periods, I delivered a short speech to calm the boys down and avoid any sort of panic setting in. As team captain, I told the guys that we had to go back out there and fire on all cylinders! I felt that my pep talk had worked. As we were getting ready to leave the dressing room, our coach walked in, concern written all over his face. He gave an incoherent speech that was delivered so nervously that we felt completely deflated. We lost our mojo, the game, then the series. I always wondered how much the coach's behavior influenced the game's outcome.

Human beings are social beings, just as much at work as during a hockey game. We find ourselves in groups all the time, so it's normal to be influenced by the energy of our peers. We just need to be aware of this social influence and, when we can, choose situations that are beneficial for us. If this isn't possible, then put a shield on so that you're not consumed by the negative influences around you to the detriment of your own positivism.

I was the mental performance coach for five athletes during the Rio Olympics. One of them was Canadian decathlete Damian Warner. The decathlon consists of ten events over two days: three throwing events, three jumping events, and four running events. Athletes earn points based on results for each event, and the one who accumulates the most points is crowned champion. Decathletes are rarely perfect in all ten events. There are at least a few unexpected hiccups, so it's common to ride an emotional roller coaster over the course of the competition.

To support Damian, the other coaches and I agreed to display a positive attitude no matter what happened. We promised each other that we would stay confident and unshakeable when Damian experienced moments of doubt. The moment would certainly come, we just didn't know when. Even if Damian had learned stress management techniques, we knew he was counting on us for additional support. Heading into the Olympic Games, we knew that beating the great American champion Ashton Eaton was a long shot. Not impossible, but unlikely.

Fast-forward to day two. The first eight events had gone reasonably well, but far below Damian's own expectations. Not only was the gold medal beyond his reach, but he also had to give up the silver because of Frenchman Kevin Mayer's impressive performance. As Damian was getting ready for the ninth event, he had to accept that he was now fighting for bronze against Germany's Kai Kazmirek.

This was the moment we were prepared and waiting for.

The ninth event is the javelin throw. The athlete is allowed three attempts to throw the javelin as far as possible. Kazmirek's best throw out of three attempts was 64.6 meters (70 yards), a personal best. Damian, for his part, couldn't throw farther than 58 and 56 meters (61 and 63 yards) on his first two attempts. His back was against the wall. He needed a much better throw on his final attempt to collect valuable points and reduce the gap separating him from the German before the final event, the 1,500-meter run. At that point, Kazmirek was sitting comfortably in third place in the overall standings.

I was in the stadium, sitting in the front row with the other coaches, roughly 150 feet from Damian. He still had some time to get ready for his last javelin throw. I was watching him as he was sitting there, nervously, shoulders bent forward, with a long face and worry in his eyes. His posture didn't bode well for this decisive moment.

With a few minutes to go, he looked in our direction, acknowledged our presence, and walked over. We showed him our enthusiasm through encouraging gestures and big smiles, and shared a few last-minute technical cues. Suddenly, he realized that he wasn't alone. His face lit up, and he smiled back at us with that same grin that we knew so well.

His body language completely changed.

Damian approached his final attempt much more confidently. He threw the javelin with authority, and it finally pinned the ground at 63.2 meters (69 yards), his best throw all season! Damian ended the decathlon beautifully with a great 1,500-metre run to finish with 8,666 points, enough to beat the German and capture his first Olympic medal.

Damian did mention afterwards how important that moment was. Our positivity was contagious enough to help him change his inner chatter from "I'm worried" to "I know I can do it."

Let's put this into practice. I would like to share with you an exercise I like to call "Energy Givers and Energy Takers." The goal is to identify all the situations, people, tasks, and environments that energize you followed by the ones that drain your energy.

Once you've completed the first step, you then come up with practical strategies that will maximize the things that generate energy and minimize the things that don't. I use the verb *minimize* because only in a perfect world could we ever eliminate all the energy takers from our daily lives.

This exercise is especially useful to protect your valuable energy throughout your workday.

Here's an example based on the responses of a corporate client.

Energy Takers	Minimize?	Energy Givers	Maximize?
My boss	• better organized for shorter meetings • come in with the right attitude	Eighties music	• listen to music when doing paperwork
Sitting at my desk for long periods of time	• walk for five min. every hour	My colleague Michael	• pop into his office regularly • have lunch together
----	----	----	----
----	----	----	----
----	----	----	----

Let's start by looking at two examples of situations that drained this client's energy levels.

"My boss is moody and intimidating. I always feel apprehensive about our weekly meeting. I never want to go."

This client knew he had to give himself the means to handle this situation better. So, he decided to send his boss an agenda ahead of time so that the discussions would be structured and more efficient. By doing this, he hoped that it would shorten the meetings. He also wanted to change his frame of mind. Instead of showing up feeling completely vulnerable, only he could improve the situation by adopting a better attitude and refusing to give her all this power over him.

He also realized that staying glued to his chair all day was affecting his mood and impeding his performance. To fix this, he decided to program a timer to go off every hour. He would then get up and walk for five minutes to stretch his legs. He knew that he would be more efficient after moving for a few minutes.

Now, over to the energy givers.

"I love listening to music from the eighties. This music brings back nice memories that make me feel good," he told me.

We decided that he should connect his ear buds when he had to get through tasks that weigh him down, like paperwork.

"I really like Michael. He's ambitious, energetic, and funny."

He made it a habit to drop by Michael's office once in a while and invite him to lunch more often to chitchat about his current projects.

You, too, can find simple ways to reduce the impact of the takers while using the givers better to maximize your energy levels every day.

Have the right attitude

As a mental coach, I'm often asked which mental skill is the most important. Without a doubt, the answer is having the *right attitude*.

Olympians travel around the world to take part in different international competitions. They live out of their suitcases. Before they leave, I often ask them if they've packed the *one thing* that they can't leave behind. After they've rhymed off clothes, equipment, a pillow, and all the usual things, they no longer know what to tell me. I tell them, "Make sure you've packed the right attitude. Everything else is secondary."

The brain is a powerful tool that can help or harm you, and you're fully responsible for showing it the way. Healthy and positive thoughts, even if they don't come spontaneously, will end up conditioning the mind.

> Nothing is good or bad;
> it's only your thinking that makes it so.

In closing, here's an interesting fact about the word *attitude* that you may have already seen on your social media feeds.

First, let's assign a percentage in sequence to each of the letters of the alphabet, starting with 1 percent. For example, A = 1, B = 2, ... Z = 26. Next, let's add the percentages for each of the letters in the word A T T I T U D E:

$$a + t + t + i + t + u + d + e$$
$$1 + 20 + 20 + 9 + 20 + 21 + 4 + 5$$
$$=$$
$$100$$

Not 77, not 113, but 100 percent! Is this a coincidence? Of course! But does it make sense? Absolutely!

CHAPTER 5

Be There When It Counts

After finishing second at the Sochi Olympic Games in 2014, Canadian figure skaters Tessa Virtue and Scott Moir decided to retire from competition. Their retirement lasted all of two years before they announced their unexpected return to competition with the objective of recapturing the Olympic title that they had won at the 2010 Vancouver Olympics.

It was February 20, 2018, at the PyeongChang Olympic Games in South Korea. I was standing next to the boards, and it was now their turn to go. We hugged each other one last time before they stepped out onto the ice to perform their long program, the free dance. Tension hung in the air, all of us aware of the magnitude of this moment. The night before, they had skated their short program beautifully and sat in first place with a two-point cushion heading into the free dance.

They skated to center ice to take their positions, the last competitors to go. A hush settled over the jam-packed Gangneung Ice Arena. Their great rivals, the French skaters Gabriella Papadakis and Guillaume Cizeron, had just set a world record. Tessa and Scott knew that their performance had to be flawless for four minutes to win. They were minutes away from capturing their second individual Olympic title, and millions watched around the world.

Can you imagine the immense pressure they had to deal with? They are skating legends, they couldn't fail! Everything would be decided in a few minutes, so they had to stay focused. It was now or never.

The music began to play over the speakers. As soon as they began to skate, I knew they were dialed in. Their movements were in synch, graceful, and on point. Nothing could knock them off their game, not even the pressure of the moment. They relied on the strategies that they had practiced hundreds of times.

- They controlled their *breathing* to stay physically and mentally calm.
- They *focused* on the music to perfectly match the rhythm.
- They brought their *attention* to their feet to feel the ice and avoid overthinking.
- They *felt* each other's presence to ensure synchronicity.

They were simply indestructible. Still standing next to the boards, not moving a tad, I watched their every move, my eyes firmly fixed on them. During the performance, I felt nervous but also extremely confident. They were clearly in the zone. When athletes are in this state, they can shut everything out: the stakes, the media, the spectators, and the pressure of the moment. When that happens, Tessa and Scott are athletes on a mission who are just trusting their training and letting themselves be led by the music. Nothing more, nothing less. They're in their own world, in the *here and now*.

As the last seconds of their program ticked by, I realized that I had just witnessed one of the most beautiful Olympic performances that I had ever seen. The judges hadn't posted their scores yet, but I knew that Tessa and Scott had accomplished what they set out to do: maintain a superhuman focus within a distraction-filled situation.

Then, the scores finally showed up on the Jumbotron . . . they were crowned Olympic champions!

As they jumped for joy, I ran over to join them, hug them, and scream with them. We were all on cloud nine! Tears in my eyes, I was so happy for them. They were able to withstand all the distractions and manage the moment.

They made sure *to be there when it counted*!

Live in the present moment

Knowing how to maintain maximum focus in crucial moments is essential to performing on demand, like Olympians do at the Games. What does being *focused* mean, exactly? It's a mental skill that is required to succeed in the world of high-performance sports. No matter what the sport, coaches give cues to athletes so that they know what to focus on at any given moment during their performance.

In the workplace, however, we don't teach focusing skills enough to help workers concentrate optimally on the task at hand. We treat it like it's a skill people come by naturally, and like there aren't any distractions at work. It's a problem. Besides, we would never ask an Olympian to perform on the big stage without first mentally preparing them to do so. Realistically, they could perform well without it, but doing so would be risky, especially if their rivals had prepared well mentally.

Outside of sport, the mental skill of *concentration* is sometimes associated with Zen masters or yogis. You know, these gurus who appear so calm and poised, locked in the present moment, oblivious of any stress. Yet there's so much more to this essential mental skill.

> *Concentration* is the ability to pay attention
> to the right things at the right time while
> ignoring the distractions.

Concentrating isn't easy to do, since there are all kinds of distractions, whether on the playing field or at work. Internal factors such as hunger, fatigue, or negative thoughts can prevent us from concentrating. There are also external factors that can throw us off our game, such as phone calls, noisy crowds, buzzing notifications, or tedious tasks.

Let's get a little more specific. Fundamentally, optimal concentration is achieved with the mastery of two vital skills: the ability to *focus* on something and the ability to *maintain* that focus.

1. *Focusing* is essentially being able to pay attention to all relevant information. You can concentrate on something without paying attention to the right thing, which is, of course, inefficient. For example, your colleague could be talking to you about a project, yet, instead of listening closely to what she's telling you, you're thinking about what you're going to wear this evening for your dinner date.

Here's an analogy to help you grasp the concept a little better. When you take a photo using a traditional camera (not your smartphone), you turn the focus ring back and forth until the image appears perfectly clear, then *click*. Mental focus works the same way. The skill of focusing is adjusting our attention until the point of interest is clear, sharp, and precise.

2. Focusing on the right element is one thing, but then you need to be able to maintain it for x amount of

time, depending on how long it will take to complete the task. For example, if your ability to concentrate properly is limited to one hour, but the meeting you're in lasts ninety minutes, you're probably going to miss a few things along the way. In this case, you need to find ways to increase your ability to focus.

This is why Olympians practice endlessly before competing. Tessa and Scott repeated their program hundreds of times before winning gold in PyeongChang. Their brains were well trained to stay completely focused for four minutes.

Understanding these two elements will help you implement the concentration strategies that we'll look at more closely later in this chapter.

On, off

Maintaining extreme focus requires extreme effort. Still, we rarely have to concentrate nonstop for several hours at a time at work or anywhere else for that matter. Throughout the day, we can allow our minds to wander occasionally when we take a break, travel to see a client, walk to a meeting, or grab a coffee. We're clever enough to know that some specific moments require a lot of concentration and others don't. For example, a pilot who's about to land a plane will be locked-in, whereas a pilot cruising at high altitude can chillax.

In the sports world, the golfer playing eighteen holes doesn't need to stay focused for five hours straight. Maintaining optimal concentration takes a lot of mental energy, so golfers have to pace themselves and zone in only during key moments. A mental performance coach I know works with several PGA golfers. He told me that the typical amount of time of intense concentration on the golf course is no more than thirty seconds at a time. For a golfer that plays even par, which is typically seventy-two strokes in a round, the total amount of concentration time is approximately thirty-six minutes (30 seconds x 72 strokes = 36). Needless to say, it would require a few extra minutes for an average golfer like me!

If you watch a professional golf tournament on television, you'll see players chatting with their caddy and being fairly relaxed between shots. However, when it's time to hit the ball, the player is suddenly fully focused. To help golfers get in their zone in preparation for their next shot, I ask them to imagine a five-meter circle around the ball. The golfer starts their pre-shot routine only when they step inside that circle.

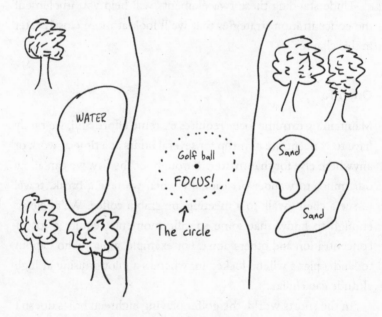

This circle helps golfers channel their focus at the right time and use the downtime between shots to unwind and save energy.

Where is your concentration circle at work? Your cubicle? The moment you walk into your office? When can you relax at work?

The attention span of a goldfish

A study published by Microsoft in 2015 reported that our attention span has dropped from twelve to eight seconds since 2000 — a 33 percent decline! Isn't that awful? The results of this study are especially staggering when you consider that a goldfish's attention span is nine seconds, which is now longer than ours!

Distractions are everywhere in our society. The sources are multiple, but mobile devices are mostly to blame. We've become dependent on these addictive little machines. They take up a huge amount of our precious time. Are we now like Pavlov's dogs, conditioned to respond to the slightest vibration or sound notification? How many times a day do we stop what we're doing to check what an alert from our phone is about? Think about how much time is lost from being distracted. If we could calculate the amount, how much does this lost time cost businesses? I'm not sure employers want to know.

Are you often disrupted by wondering,

- Who wants to talk to me?
- Is this the answer I've been waiting for?
- How many likes did I get on my last post?
- Is this urgent?

Everything seems to be urgent these days.

Let's say you're talking with your best friend, and your telephone starts to vibrate. Do you stay as focused on what your friend is saying? We often give in to curiosity, even if it's to the detriment of our close relationships.

Several trends, such as yoga, meditation, and mindfulness, suggest that we relearn how to just *be* by staying connected to the present moment. I use the verb *relearn* because we knew how to naturally stay focused when we were children. Have you ever seen a young child play with their blocks or color with their markers? They are in their own little world, as if nothing else existed. We've gone from being children living in the present to adults with the attention span of a goldfish.

We like to think that we're multitaskers, but we aren't really. *Multitasking* is a word that comes from computer engineering and is defined as the ability to process several tasks or programs at one time. Our brains aren't wired to consciously do multiple things at a time. What we as human beings do is not multitasking in the computer sense of the word, but rather just moving from one task to another in a short period of time.

Flitting from task to task doesn't improve productivity at all. What you are basically doing is disconnecting from one in order to connect to another, then disconnecting from that task to reconnect to the first one, and so on. This is nothing more than a strenuous psychological exercise filled with multiple interruptions. It also becomes a huge energy sucker. When we go back to a task that we stopped doing for a moment, we never really get back to the point where we left off. We need to put ourselves back into the situation mentally to pick up our line of thinking, losing precious energy along the way.

A more efficient way to work is to finish a task by giving it the attention it needs, rather than spread ourselves thin. The Olympian at work is in the zone only when they deliberately focus on one task at a time.

A state of heightened awareness

Human resources managers in various businesses tell me that being able to focus properly is becoming more and more of an interesting asset when it comes time to hire new employees.

Cal Newport, a computer science professor at Georgetown University in Washington, D.C., wrote a book called *Deep Work* that talks about the state of profound concentration we need to accomplish important tasks at work. Too many of us use superficial concentration, which makes it seem like we're productive because we might have finished the task in less time, but the quality is often questionable as a result. Likewise, mistakes made in the workplace are often because of a lack of deep concentration.

Unfortunately, this mental skill is a resource that is becoming scarce in a world filled with distractions. It's become one of the reasons employers like to hire former high-level athletes: they've already mastered the skill of zoning in when it comes time to perform. The sports world teaches us that to reach this state of optimal concentration, we first have to limit the distractions within the performance environment. To be *in the zone* can't be forced. Instead, it happens naturally when the environment no longer poses a threat to our ability to concentrate.

My colleague Angus Mugford, vice-president of high performance with the Toronto Blue Jays, saw it firsthand while working on his doctoral thesis. He studied the way high-level rowers were able to find this zone, also called the *flow state*. Among several factors in reaching this zone, the most decisive aspect his results showed was finding an environment in which very few things could potentially distract the athletes.

I, too, had the chance to witness this among some of the athletes I work with. The successful Olympians were so good at managing their environment, probably because they perceived the competitive context as positive, constructive, and conducive to performing well.

We have no control over what comes our way, but we have full control over how we interpret it.

When I train Olympians, I make sure they can recognize when they've become distracted so they can quickly regain control. Self-awareness is arguably one of the most important mental skills to have in your toolbox. Of course, athletes can become distracted, but the best ones aren't disturbed for very long, as they are extremely aware of their mental state at any given time.

While working on this book at my kitchen table, my computer could easily distract me. To find my flow state, I decided to deactivate every possible notification and pop-up window. I closed Skype, and I put my smartphone on silent and purposefully placed it out of reach. The kids were at school, the house was quiet! Some mornings, I would go to the gym to get some endorphins flowing to make sure my brain was on. With no distractions, I was completely focused on what I wanted to write. I was *on fire*.

Control your environment

Over the last few years, I've been facilitating mental training workshops for Osedea, a tech company specializing in mobile apps and other digital products. In this line of work, programmers need sharp concentration skills to do their jobs optimally.

I challenged the company to find new ways to increase efficiency, productivity, and, ultimately, profitability. The managers were up for the challenge and came up with a new company concept called *sterile cockpit,* a practice borrowed from the aviation world. The U.S. Federal Aviation Administration (FAA) introduced the Sterile Cockpit Rule in 1981 for all flight personnel whose tasks required optimal concentration during the most delicate operations, such as takeoff and landing. Essentially, any task that was not directly related to these operations was prohibited, including conversations between crew members. The rule had become necessary following a series of accidents resulting from distracted crew members inside the cockpit during these delicate in-flight operations.

Osedea decided to put this concept to the test. From Monday to Thursday between 1:30 p.m. and 3:00 p.m., the programmers block off all types of interactions — no phone calls, no emails, no texting, no talking with work colleagues — to focus entirely on one project for ninety minutes. Their efficiency rate increased considerably. By getting rid of distractions to such an extent, the programmers were able to reach their full potential so much more easily. The concept has turned out to be so efficient that the programmers unanimously decided that they can't work without it now.

Another company that I work with decided to ban smartphones during meetings. It's so common these days to see colleagues show up in the meeting room, their noses glued to their phones, until everyone has arrived. For some, the temptation of looking at their device during a meeting is too strong. It's not unusual to see the same behavior everywhere, whether in a restaurant, a waiting room, or on the street.

Team meetings for this company are crucial moments during which brilliant ideas can emerge and employee collaboration can shine. During a discussion with the management team, I was explaining to them how smartphones can hinder meeting productivity. Using sports analogies, I pointed out that tennis players never look at their phones between points, and hockey players never send text messages between their shifts on the bench. The CEO got such a kick out of these stories that he decided to act and eliminate mobile devices.

Bye-bye, distractions

By now, you'll have understood that one of the most important strategies to enhance performance levels is as simple as eliminating, or at least significantly reducing, any form of distraction to allow the brain to focus on the task at hand. I used the following equation to illustrate the principle:

$$\text{Potential} - \text{Distractions} = \text{Level of Performance}$$

Let's add some numbers to better understand the equation. Let's say your potential is worth 100 percent, since it's a value that you can control and tap into at any given time. In other words, you have the potential to reach the best version of yourself 100 percent of the time.

For example, you arrive at the office one morning after having slept poorly and passing on breakfast, feeling stressed about the meeting scheduled for later that day. Let's give these distractions a value of 50 percent. Obviously, your performance level will suffer because of them, so it won't be greater than 50 percent.

$$\text{Potential} - \text{Distractions} = \text{Level of Performance}$$
$$100\% - 50\% = 50\%$$

Still, if you were able to minimize the distractions by using the strategies that I'll be suggesting a little later in this chapter, you'll come close to reaching your full potential.

$$\text{Potential} - \text{Distractions} = \text{Level of Performance}$$
$$100\% - 35\% = 65\%$$
$$100\% - 10\% = 90\%$$

Mental performance coaching is not a common profession, therefore, not many people know about it. So, when people ask me what I do for a living, I often use this equation as a metaphor to help people understand a big part of my job. I get my clients to ignore the possible distractions and, ultimately, eliminate them completely from their workday. Really, my role is to help individuals achieve optimal performance by *unlocking* their potential.

With snowboarder Max Parrot, we eliminated many distractions to enable him to tap into his world-class potential and improve his chances of winning every time he competes. In addition to the challenge of the course, there are so many elements that could throw him off: the buzzing crowd, the risk of injury, the reporters, the prize money, and the gold medal. Just before he's about to take off, he does a little housekeeping to allow his mind to connect with the present moment. Everything is clear. He's in the zone. He is focused to the max.

Take a moment to think about your work environment and review the following questions, which may help you see things more clearly.

- Small or big, what distractions do you face daily?
- Are they cutting into your potential? If yes, by how much: 25%, 30%, 60%?
- Are they difficult to reduce or eliminate completely?
- Do you have the necessary discipline to minimize these distractions? Do you need help?
- Could you benefit from a concentration-booster concept such as the *sterile cockpit*?

Take up the challenge. Use the suggested means wisely to get closer to reaching your full potential.

Time stands still

Imagine going through a workday when you don't have to immediately respond to an unending stream of emails, text messages, or any other tasks that demand your attention. Now, think about a task in which you were so caught up you didn't notice time passing; you're in harmony with the present moment, time just seems to be standing still. You have the impression of being all alone, of feeling completely in sync with the moment. We usually enjoy these moments, and they do us good.

I experience these eureka moments when I have both hands buried in the wet soil of my garden or when I'm playing a favorite sport. The same thing happens in my professional life when I give talks. I don't think of anything other than what's happening. I'm completely immersed, sharing this special feeling with the participants, who have taken the time to come and listen.

The best athletes are regularly *in the zone* whether they're training or competing. During a training camp in beautiful Zermatt, Switzerland, freestyle skier Mikaël Kingsbury and I agreed to meet for dinner at 7:00 p.m. at the favorite local cheese fondue restaurant. Training had ended at 2:00, and Mikaël would be spending the rest of the afternoon going over training videos, catching up with his family via Skype, and taking a nap.

I was craving Swiss cheese when I arrived a little early at the restaurant, at 6:55 p.m. Mik was nowhere to be seen. I waited and waited, but still no Mik. Finally, at 7:35 p.m., I saw the world champion run through the entrance door and approach our table. Out of breath, he mumbled, "JF . . . I'm . . . so sorry . . . that . . . I'm late!" I joked that the nap must have been a little longer than planned. He replied that he wasn't late because of the nap, but rather that he'd been watching training videos all afternoon and had completely lost track of time.

Time flies when we're having fun! Great champions are so passionate about their sport, getting anchored in the present moment is not a chore, it's simply a habit.

I hope that you, too, get to experience the sense of time standing still at work.

Our floating head

What follows are a few images that will help you understand this principle of the floating head better.

Do you agree that, if we want to perform well, the mind and the body must work together in harmony, as shown by the stick man below? I assume yes.

Would you also agree that, if the mind is distracted by past or future situations, it won't be able to stay firmly grounded in the present and will struggle to focus on what's currently going on? Yes? Okay, let's keep going.

When our bodies move, they do so in the present moment, right? If I hit a ball, I'm doing it in the here and now. If I raise my hand to ask a question, I'm doing it right at that moment. Our bodies always act in the moment, just like our stick man here.

PRESENT

While the body is always in the present moment, the brain, on the other hand, is the only part that can be in the present, the past, or future. In this next image, the stick man's head is in the past.

- Frustration
- Anger
- Annoyance

PAST   PRESENT

Let's consider this example on a golf course. Our stick man is about to tee off on the third hole. His body is there, searching for the right stance as he gets ready to drive the ball off the tee. But his head is back on the second hole, still ruminating on that darn triple bogey. Three strokes over par hurts! During that moment, he feels frustrated, angry, and annoyed. His mind is incapable of letting go of that bad second hole and remains stuck in the past, while his body is on the next hole — not good!

In this scenario, the head and body are worlds apart, unable to work in harmony. What's even worse, the head will most likely transfer the frustration from the second hole to the third hole, which hasn't been played yet. "I played so badly at the last hole. What will this one be like? A little too far to the right, I'll get caught in the sand trap. A little too far to the left, and I'll be in the bushes. Urgh!" Our stick man feels nothing but concern, fear, and nervousness.

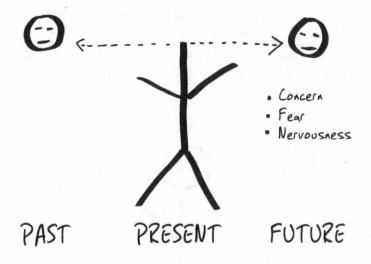

PAST   PRESENT   FUTURE

As a result, his head is floating between the past and the future. Unsettled by the mind's negative inner chatter, the muscles begin to tense up, and the body mechanics become jerky. Our stick man isn't able to pay enough attention to the target in front of him because he is too preoccupied with the possibility of playing another bad hole. He hits the ball, but the chances of making a good shot are rather slim.

Do you golf? Perhaps you recognize yourself here? We're all victims of this disconnection between head and body at one time or another, whether at work, at home, or while playing our favorite sport.

Why do we have so much trouble keeping our brains firmly attached to our bodies? Why do our brains tend to wander back and forth between the past and the future during stressful moments? It's a normal reaction given that our protective brains want to avoid reliving unpleasant situations.

On the one hand, it isn't bad if our brains want to protect us, as we can learn from our mistakes and correct our behavior. It's also beneficial to think ahead to prepare for a future event in an optimal way. Yet when it's crucial to capture all the information we need to perform, the head and the body have to align. Think about when you're driving a car. You remain alert to even the slightest detail that could affect your safety. Your body is also alert, ready to react, to press the brakes quickly or swerve to avoid an obstacle in the road.

PRESENT

Being grounded in the present is a skill, and, like any skill, it takes work to develop. The mind naturally wanders, so if we rarely train our heads and our bodies to work together, our heads will float between the past and the future. This headspace will become habit and far too familiar to us. If you've tried yoga or meditation, you'll know that it's challenging to remain in the present moment right from the very first session; but with practice, you can get there.

After being exposed to the stick man principle, my clients say that they catch themselves with their head in the past or the future when, ideally, it needed to be in the present moment. I'm guessing that from now on you, too, will become more aware of the divide between your head and your body. Being able to catch yourself is a very important first step.

With purposeful training, it can become totally natural to align head and body. Do you remember the old video games in which we had to collect energy capsules to strengthen our lives? In the same vein, I want to share with you three strategies that will reinforce the connection. You'll notice that these strategies all have one thing in common: they draw your attention to your body for the simple reason that, like we said earlier, the body is *always* in the present.

Breathe

Breathing. Is there anything more fundamental than breathing for survival? We do it without even thinking about it.

But how good of a breather are you?

The common denominator among all relaxation and mind-fulness techniques — yoga, meditation, tai chi — is breathing. Why does breathing systematically allow us to reconnect with the present moment? Because we don't breathe with our heads!

Breathing is a physiological (body) exercise, a collaboration between the diaphragm and the lungs that supplies oxygen to the human body. As a result, bringing our attention to our breath is bringing our attention to our body in the now.

> Breathing connects our heads with our bodies because we don't breathe in the past or in the future, we only breathe in the present moment.

Try the following exercise. First, take a few seconds to think about yesterday. Picture your day again in your mind.

Next, take a few seconds to think about your day tomorrow and visualize your upcoming activities.

Now, take a deep breath while you read these lines. Inhale s-l-o-w-l-y to fill your lungs. Feel your chest and belly expand. You've got it. Now, exhale.

Again. Take a deep breath and feel your lungs expand, then empty. One last time: take a long, deep breath, then release. While you were focused on your breathing, were you thinking about your day yesterday or about what's coming up tomorrow? Probably not.

Elite athletes constantly rely on breathing techniques, especially at crucial moments during a competition. The basketball player before a free throw, the gymnast before mounting the balance beam, the skier before setting off down the course, the soccer player before a penalty kick — we see them take a deep breath, exhale, then execute their performance.

When boxer Marie-Ève Dicaire walks back to her corner at the end of a round, her heart is beating a hundred miles an hour, and she's usually out of breath. At this time, her coach, Stéphane Harnois, has one minute to give her some important feedback based on what just happened so that she keeps applying the original plan, or sometimes there are some adjustments to be made. To make sure she's listening, he gives her time to take a few deep breaths, even before saying a word, so that she connects with the present moment and becomes more attentive to his feedback. Her head is in the here and now, not in the round that just ended or in the round about to start.

At work, how often do you use mindful breathing? This skill prevents your head from floating all over the place. We'll talk more about the benefits of breathing and how to master it in the next chapter.

Use your senses

In recent years, I've worked with elite track and field athletes. One of them was a sprinter who wanted to improve his starts, especially in the 100-meter race. His start out of the blocks lacked explosiveness, and he felt that he was losing some valuable hundredths of a second. Given my limited experience in the sport, I asked him a series of questions to better understand what he needed to do while he was in the starting blocks.

"What do you think about when you're in the blocks, ready to start?" I asked.

"I'm waiting for the starter pistol to fire," he replied.

One word caught my attention: *waiting*.

For this athlete, waiting meant trying to anticipate when the gun would fire. This can cause problems because, if the starting signal didn't happen exactly as anticipated, the body can be out of sync coming out of the blocks and lose precious time. The brain is in the future during the process of *waiting* (i.e., "Is the pistol shot coming?"). Humans don't like to wait; we would rather be *there* already. Think about the moment you stand in line at the supermarket, waiting for your turn to pay for your groceries. You would really prefer to be paying already, right?

His attention wasn't focused on the right thing. Given that his brain was trying to anticipate, he wasn't completely in the present moment. So, when the gun fired, his brain would have had to understand that now is the moment to jump out of the blocks and relay that information to the body. It's a matter of a few hundredths of a second, but in a 100-meter dash, that can be the difference between first and fourth place.

To counter this, while he was in the blocks and ready to go, I suggested that he simply *listen*, relying only on his hearing. It seemed to me that, with his extensive experience, he no longer needed to tell his body to jump out of the blocks when he *heard* the gunshot. My hypothesis was that his body would immediately react on its own to the slightest noise because his body was trained to do just that.

This change paid off. He was able to shave a few hundredths of a second off his starts and, more importantly, become more consistent from one race to the next.

Our senses are physiological mechanisms whose main functions are to pick up information and transmit it to the brain. The senses always operate in the present.

Below is an exercise to help you put this principle into practice.

Sit comfortably. Take a moment to simply *look* around you. Pay particular attention to the details of the room: shapes, colors, and the distance between objects. Next, take the time to *listen*. Do you hear any ambient noises, such as an aircraft flying overhead, voices in the background, the dishwasher, or the fridge? Maybe total silence? Now, *feel* your body sitting on the chair, lying in bed, or lounging on the sofa. Feel your back being supported. Feel your legs and your feet.

During this short moment, you were in the present moment.

Our senses are just as useful at work. When you chat with a colleague, how well are you listening? Are you listening to what they're saying to be able to *respond* or to *understand*? If you're listening to respond, you're only waiting for your turn to speak without really concentrating on what they're saying. But when we listen to understand, we're using our senses wisely. We pay attention to what is being said, the tone of voice, the choice of words, and the body language. All this information being captured enables us to really understand what the person is telling us.

It's impressive how many details we do pick up when we're really using our senses correctly. For example, on the next page is an image of my Timex sports watch. I drew the image of my watch on the left spontaneously without taking the time to look at it before starting. On the right is a drawing that I did after looking at it carefully for thirty seconds. The hundreds of times that I've looked at it in the past month apparently made no difference. It was only after looking at it attentively for half a minute that I was able to capture all the details.

If you were to do the same exercise, you'd come up with two different drawings, too. Now, what would happen if we were to apply this exercise to our daily lives?

How many times do we just glance at the details, rather than examine them closely? Are you able to remember discussions you were barely tuned in to, rather than the ones when you were actually listening to what was being said?

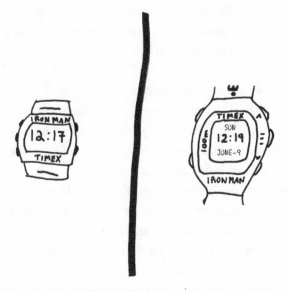

I constantly challenge Mikaël Kingsbury to really *look* at the moguls when he skies them. I applied the same technique to skaters Tessa Virtue and Scott Moir by asking them to really *listen* to the music during their performance and to *feel* each other's presence to remain perfectly synchronized. With world champion high jumper Derek Drouin, it's a question of really *staring* at the bar so that his body records the thrust it will take to clear it. Judoka Antoine Valois-Fortier must pay particular attention to his sense of *proprioception* (awareness of the position and movement of the body) to be well placed to lay down a strategic attack.

When hockey goalies are confident and focused, they *see* everything that's coming their way. Using your senses properly leads to a heightened state of awareness. When goaltenders are in this state, the puck looks as big as a beach ball, and they know they're in the zone.

Using your senses connects you with the now. So, train your senses! Take some time, each day, to pay attention to your senses to capture some of the details that you normally miss. This ability will improve over time and will serve you well at work.

The best coaches and leaders are very good at paying attention. Being attentive means using the senses optimally to grasp a situation and better understand a discussion.

Give yourself simple instructions

You've surely heard of the acronym KISS, which stands for "keep it simple, stupid." We have every interest in keeping our explanations, feedback, and comments as simple and as concrete as possible so that we're understood.

If the coach says to the golfer, "Keep your head stable, make sure your feet are firmly planted on the ground, turn the hips, don't hold the club too tightly, and remember to complete the swing," that would be far too much information. In this case, the athlete may fall victim to *analysis paralysis*. Too much information causes the athlete to tense up and become stuck in their thoughts. Struggling to stay in the present moment, their movements typically become out of sync and erratic.

Imagine a boss who gives their employee instructions just before they're to meet with a client. "Stay calm. Don't comment too directly. Tell him to be more on time for meetings. Try to establish trust with him. Make him laugh and don't prolong the meeting for no reason." Yikes — too much information!

The best sports coaches are masters of the KISS principle. When it's time to give some feedback, they make an effort to choose one or two precise nuggets, not more. It's useless to list a ton of reminders just before the golfer is about to swing when all that's needed is to emphasize feeling the rhythm and keeping an eye on the ball. Nothing more, nothing less. As Michel Hamelin, Mikaël Kingsbury's moguls skiing coach, says, "The more you say, the more it gets diluted." We should never water down key words.

The same principle applies to the conversation you have with yourself. Your brain is made to think. Switching it off is next to impossible. Even when you decide to slow it down, thoughts will find the cracks and will surface. It's better to give your brain short and precise instructions in the first place, rather than trying to filter your thoughts when you notice the overload.

High-level athletes plan their way of thinking ahead of time, especially in preparation for upcoming stressful moments, as emotions can easily cloud the brain. Because of it, they can use the key words that they chose ahead of time so that their attention is focused on the right thing during the critical moments. Nothing is left to chance.

Professional dart players are a very good example. With players standing seven feet, nine inches away from the board, the objective of the game is to be the first player to get rid of all the 501 points assigned to each player at the beginning of the game. Different areas on the board are worth specific amounts of points, so every target hit is deducted from the player's total score. The best bang for your buck is pinning triple 20 (worth sixty points), an area approximately one square inch in size. Needless to say, extreme precision is an essential skill in this sport. The areas that border triple 20 are triple 5 (fifteen points) and triple 1 (three points). In other words, if a dart is thrown a few millimeters too far to the left or to the right, the points collected will be significantly lower.

Not only do experienced dart players look at the target, but they also tell their brain where they want the dart to go. As they get ready to throw the dart, you can read some of the players' lips as they say words like "triple 20." They whisper a clear and concise mental intention that is relayed to the body, specifically the arms and the fingers, to perform accordingly.

I encourage athletes to choose *feel words*, or reminders that relate to the physical sensation of the movement. For example, I suggest words like *feet* or *glide* to help a figure skater focus their attention on connecting with the ice, or *breathe deeply* to the golfer who wants to relax before they swing. These kinds of words help athletes loosen up their muscles and stay grounded in the present moment.

During situations that aggravate our negative emotions, such as anxiety and nervousness, our brain is searching to hang on to a reference point, like a buoy in choppy waters. If we don't plan this safety net ahead of time, our brain will scramble to pick one anyways, and the end result will most likely not be pretty. You may have already experienced this situation during a crisis at work, when you quickly lose your bearings.

One of my clients is a department manager who often turns to reminders to help her achieve peak performance at work. Below are a few examples:

- During team meetings, she reminds herself to look her colleagues in the eye when speaking to them. Through visual contact, she wants to convey that she values their presence and considers them important members of her team.
- When having to deal with tough situations, she's aware of her tendency to become socially awkward. She typically squirms on her chair and begins speaking faster. The key words that she chose were *sit up straight* and *speak slowly*.

Be creative! Choose specific reminders that work for you. Athletes often write them on their stick, their racket, or their glove as a reminder. At the office, you can use your personal bulletin board, computer screen, or notebook.

The KISS principle should include the word *smart* instead of *stupid*: keep it simple and *smart*. In the end, having key words to rely on enables us to act more intelligently, especially when managing challenging situations, and is another skill essential for becoming an Olympian at work.

Types of attention

I have to admit, I don't remember everything I learned during my eight years at university. However, one thing I do remember from my first sports psychology class is a theoretical model created by

Dr. Robert Nideffer. He's a world-renowned psychologist who has written several books and worked with top athletes, business-people, and army personnel in the United States. His model is straightforward and easy to implement with my clients. Hopefully it will be as useful for you as it is for me.

Earlier in this chapter, I explained that there were two important elements to grasp to ensure proper concentration: the ability to *focus* on something and the ability to *maintain* that focus. Well, Nideffer's model has to do with the former. He defines four *attentional styles* to determine what type of focus is best to use according to the task.

1. *Internal attention*: we pay attention to details inside us, such as focusing on our breathing.
2. *External attention*: we pay attention to details outside us, such as concentrating on reading a book.
3. *Narrow attention*: we pay attention to one detail at a time, such as a conversation with one person.
4. *Broad attention*: we pay attention to several details at a time, such as when we're driving.

Nideffer arranged the different attentional styles into a quadrant, which provides four possible combinations: narrow-internal, broad-internal, narrow-external, and broad-external.

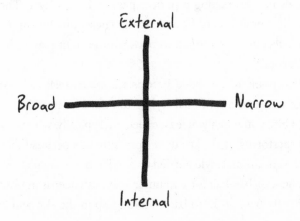

First, let's use a few sporting examples to put the model into practice. Then, we'll look at how to use it in the workplace. You'll quickly notice that different situations call for different combinations.

Let's go through a golfer's pre-shot routine. He walks onto the tee box, club in hand. He stands roughly twelve feet behind the ball to analyze the course in front of him: sand trap 185 yards away, water on the left, trees to the right, etcetera (broad-external). His plan is to hit the ball along the left side of the fairway to get into a good position for his second shot (broad-external). The golfer now chooses the exact spot he wants to drive the ball (narrow-external), takes a deep breath (narrow-internal), and stares even harder at that precise target (narrow-external). While looking at his spot, he visualizes the ball's trajectory (narrow-internal). Then, the golfer calmly walks towards the ball, positions himself correctly over it (broad-external), and wiggles his body gently to make sure he's loose (broad-internal). He never takes his eyes off the ball during the entire swing (narrow-external), and . . . *ping!* Within approximately twenty-five seconds, the golfer needed to switch seven times between all four different attentional combinations to execute his drive. No wonder golfing is so mental!

Golf is one example, but there are several other sports that require multiple combinations of attentional styles. For example, a football quarterback has to process a ton of information in a few seconds before making a perfect pass to his receiver. The same goes for a point guard in basketball. These athletes' brains need to be exceptionally trained to perform the right play in fractions of a second.

The point to be made here is that each task can require a whole range of attentional styles. You need to consider this or it might bite you when you least expect it. Typically, when an athlete underperforms or chokes under pressure, it's because they don't use the attentional style needed to handle that particular moment.

Think of baseball for a minute. The outfielder is in position to catch a fly ball, his head back, looking up in the sky, and his eyes focused on the approaching ball. It's a routine play for pros. But even the pros mess up from time to time, and this player ends up dropping the fly ball (probably due to a lack of narrow-external focus). What happens next is compelling. Panicking, the outfielder scrambles to pick up the ball off the ground and throw it to the intended teammate. In theory, this player should allocate narrow-external attention to his throw, but it's highly probable that his blunder is preventing him from focusing properly. The end result? The player throws the ball ten feet off target because his negative inner chatter took over. "You're such an idiot!" Clearly, broad-internal focus was engaged instead of narrow-external focus.

Did you ever think different attentional styles would have such a big impact on performance?

Nideffer's model really helped Mikaël Kingsbury perform better during his dual moguls event, in which two skiers descend the course at the same time. In the individual event, Mikaël is alone on the course, which makes it easy enough to maintain a narrow-external attentional style. However, when he has a racer next to him, he can hear and feel his opponent, and see him in his peripheral vision. It would be a costly mistake to stray from his plan and start paying attention to his opponent. He needs to keep his attention narrow to focus on *his* course and *his* line of descent.

When prepping for a competition, we always take a moment to pinpoint the situations in which Mik may lose the right attentional style. We identify scenarios in which he could potentially get distracted, like peeking at his opponent ripping the course faster than he is. To avoid falling into the trap, he visualizes himself returning to the right attentional style so that, if it ever happens for real, his brain is trained to respond accordingly. I'll explain how to use visualization properly in the next chapter.

Now, let's leave the snowy slopes and switch to the workplace. The image that follows depicts a situation that one of my clients, a sales manager, experienced a few years ago. Imagine that you have to lead a meeting with twenty sales representatives to discuss the goals for the year ahead. You start off by welcoming everyone, then you scan the room to make eye contact with each individual (external-broad). You ensure that you're sitting tall, in an open and welcoming posture (internal-broad). When your colleagues speak, you pay attention to what they're saying (external-narrow) and then you listen closely to comprehend a complex question asked about last year's sales strategies (external-narrow). You take a few seconds to reflect and assess a few scenarios in your head (internal-broad) to decide on the most relevant response (internal-narrow) before explaining it to the group (external-broad). Well played.

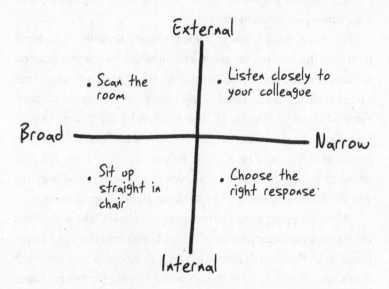

Now, let's suppose you feel vulnerable that day and, instead of using the internal-narrow attentional style to respond to your colleague's question about last year's strategies, you choose an internal-broad type focus that leads to self-doubt. "But why is he asking me that? He wants to box me in in front of everyone. If my answer is awkward, I'm going to lose face." It could very well be that, at that precise moment, your body language is betraying you, and your discomfort is visible for all to see. You start to fumble your words like the baseball player who failed to make the play.

What can cause your attention to wander? Under what circumstances should you use the different attentional styles to concentrate better? Take some time to think about this, as you may be able to identify the reasons why you become so easily distracted at work. No matter what your role is — project manager, teacher, security guard — be aware of Nideffer's model and use it accordingly.

As you can see, being an Olympian at work isn't all that different from being an elite athlete. Concentrating like an Olympian means paying attention to the right things at the right time.

Focus like an Olympian

To improve and excel, we need strategies for optimal focus, just like elite athletes do. The following are some easy-to-use techniques that Olympians implement to ignore distractions and stay connected.

Stay calm

People often tell someone who is too agitated or nervous to calm down. This advice is more appropriate than it first appears. Elite athletes must be able to calm their minds to avoid overthinking in crucial moments.

When they're in the zone, performers have quiet minds even if their bodies may be moving fast. In this surreal mental state, very few thoughts cross their minds. Some will say that they don't think about anything at all. In reality, there's cognitive reasoning going on, but they're so in tune with their bodies that they feel like their minds are empty.

It's true that, in this state of mind, their brain is not weighed down with useless thoughts. The Japanese call this state *mushin*, meaning empty mind or no thoughts. The head is fully engaged but completely free of superficial thoughts, such as concerns, worries, or fears, that could lead to intrusive emotions. As simple as it may seem, one of the best strategies to control your mind is to just slow down the brain's cognitive activity. Everything then becomes clear, enabling you to regain control of the situation. Figure skater Scott Moir used to tell me, "I make sure that the competition goes at my speed."

During a typical day, I can squeeze in seven coaching sessions. The other day I started with an early-riser corporate leader, followed by a track and field sprinter, a circus clown, a pop singer, a freestyle skier, and then a surgeon, and I finished the day with a pro hockey player. You can just imagine the variety of conversations I have in a day. It's so much fun! But one trap that I have to watch out for is bringing thoughts from one session to another. Thankfully, I created a routine that I live by to prevent this from happening.

I have the privilege of working from home, so when clients arrive at my front door, I greet them, accompany them to my office, invite them to sit comfortably, and offer them something to drink. Then I let them settle in for a few minutes by themselves. During this time, I walk into the next room, sit comfortably, and use mindful breathing for a brief moment to clear my mind and refresh completely for my next client. I flush all useless thoughts from my brain, including the previous coaching sessions, emails, text messages, or anything else that could potentially bother me. I do this to offer what matters most to my client: *my full attention*. When I walk back to my office, I'm usually in a flow state and ready to go!

Mental fogginess reminds me of the old television sets with antennas. Are you old enough to remember rabbit ears? If the antenna wasn't pointing the right way, there was interference: the sound crackled, and the picture was blurry. We had to find the position that picked up the correct airwaves and only then could we enjoy our favorite sitcom. Well, that's basically how I feel during my short relaxation routine, moving from blurry thoughts to a crystal-clear mind.

During my Cirque du Soleil days, I coached a juggler who had developed a similar technique. Before stepping out onto the stage, he would stand alone in the wings and take a minute to refocus, calm his mind, and eliminate all superficial thoughts. In his case, that minute went like what follows. I encourage you to try it.

Standing with his feet shoulder-width apart, his arms dangling at his sides, and his eyes closed,

- he inhaled three times, deeply and slowly;
- he focused his attention on his feet planted firmly on the ground;
- he let his body sway gently to the right, then forward, to the left, then backward before finally returning to a centered position; and
- he took three more deep breaths, then imagined that he had flushed his useless thoughts down the toilet and watched them swirl before they disappeared.

He topped off the routine with two call-and-responses. "What time is it?" *Now.* "Where am I?" *Here.* Then, he opened his eyes and murmured, "Showtime."

Juggling requires exceptional coordination and dexterity. This exercise helped him rebalance his nervous system and find an optimal state, both mentally and physically.

Physiologically, our bodies are activated by the nervous system. It's easier to concentrate when our nerves aren't too active. That's why slow breathing is a powerful tool. It stimulates the parasympathetic system, which is responsible for lowering the heart rate and slowing down the neurological activity in our bodies.

I encourage you to develop a short and simple relaxation technique that you'll be able to use at any time to calm your nerves, flush your mind, and get into a flow state.

"Sensalization"

You won't find the word *sensalization* in any dictionary; I made it up. Let me explain.

Visualization is a mental skill that athletes use to prepare for a competition. They imagine themselves executing their performance in the best way possible to train their brains for the challenge ahead. You may have noticed that when a downhill skier visualizes their descent, their bodies move as they imagine themselves ripping the course. They lean forward, tilt to the left, then to the right, as if they were skiing around the gates. The mental images are sent to the muscles through the nervous system to reinforce the neurological connection between the mind and the body.

Try this: close your eyes and imagine your fingers typing on a computer keyboard without actually doing it. Eventually, you'll feel a tingling sensation in your fingers. Visualization is powerful enough to create innervation from the brain all the way to your fingertips.

When the time comes to actually compete, athletes who frequently use visualization experience a feeling of déjà vu — a feeling as if they had already been in this situation before. It helps to get in the zone right from the get-go. This mental skill is even more effective when the athlete imagines the same elements that they'll find on-site, such as the competition venue, ambient sounds, opponents, and the crowd.

The word sensalization came to me during a course at university. I found that the existing term, *visualization* (also called *mental imagery*), wasn't enough. The word *visual* in visualization refers mostly to the sense of sight. The goal of visualization is to simulate, as much as possible, what will happen in real life. Given that *real* performances demand that we use all our senses, it made no sense to refer to this mental skill solely as visual. That's why I came up with the word sensalization.

This important mental skill is multisensorial, so sensalization reminds my clients to add in all the rest of their senses when they visualize something.

Here are a few important pointers so that you, too, can sensalize properly:

- *Quantify* the importance of each sense that you'll need to perform the task. For example, a police officer told me that during a dangerous operation, sight was number one (50%), followed by hearing (25%), touch (15%), smell (9%), and taste (1%). As a result, when he sensalizes different scenarios, he attributes the importance that every sense deserves.
- *Calm down* before using sensalization. Sensalizing requires a lot of concentration and energy, so it's not the type of training that we can do when highly agitated. Taking a few deep breaths is useful to start the sensalization session with a clean slate. Before giving a talk, I always show up early to look at the room to commit it to memory. Next, I spend time alone in a quiet corner backstage, to meditate and to sensalize myself being on fire.
- The secret of effective sensalization is to *do a little at a time, but often.* Since the exercise is demanding, let's emphasize quality, not quantity. Brief fifteen- to thirty-second sequences are the most effective. This is like building any good habit: if you do it often enough, it'll become second nature.

Have some intention in your attention

Have you heard of *deliberate practice*, a concept developed by Swedish psychologist and researcher K. Anders Ericsson? The fundamental premise of deliberate practice is that you must challenge yourself purposefully if you want to grow and reach performance excellence. We must have precise goals, challenge our weaknesses, and leave our comfort zones regularly.

To help them get better and stay focused, I ask hockey players to identify two or three precise goals for their game. That way, whether the game goes well or not, they can always come back to their specific objectives. These goals, which are typically things they want to improve, could be something like *get a shot on net every time you can* or *generate some speed in the neutral zone*. The player can think about these goals before the game, on the bench, or between periods.

> Beware! Your mind will focus on what you decide to pay attention to. What you focus on expands.

Have you already been told to focus, or maybe you've suggested it to your children? It isn't the best feedback to give because it's too vague. We can't concentrate optimally if we don't know what to pay attention to, right? The next time your boss, a colleague, or someone else asks you to *focus*, ask them, "On what?"

Set up a routine

You probably already know this, but elite athletes go through a specific step-by-step warm-up routine before a competition. Their warm-ups include a series of exercises that are executed in a well-thought-out sequence to prepare the body and the mind for the challenge ahead.

Let's take judo as an example. A judoka might start with a light jog to increase their heart rate and warm up their muscles, then move on to dynamic stretching to loosen up their bodies, followed by going over technical judo moves, and then finish off with a few fight simulations. Throughout this entire progression, they take brief moments here and there to focus on their breathing to reduce nervousness. Sensalization exercises are also part of the routine to review the tactical plan to win the fight. It's only after completing all these steps that the athlete is ready to face their opponent.

Warm-up routines are not improvised. The coaching staff prepare it in such a way that the judoka can step onto the tatami and feel that they're in an optimal mental and physical state. The routine is built logically so that the athlete starts with general physical exercises and then switches to technical and tactical elements specific to judo. I call this the *funnel principle*, as everything funnels down, from general to specific, towards the fight.

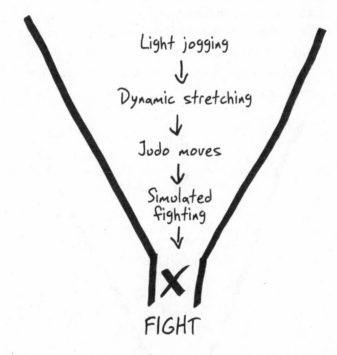

I've been providing mental performance coaching to the vice-president of a major corporation for some time now. He spends long hours in front of his computer and on his phone, sometimes both at the same time. He says that he's an expert at putting out fires, so much so that he's thinking of changing his title to *Corporate Firefighter* on his business card. When things heat up, he's often the one who needs to make quick decisions that can have major consequences for the business. So, to increase mental awareness and avoid making mistakes, he created a short routine that he uses before firing off emails and phone calls. His warm-up routine looks like this:

1. He *walks* around the building for a few minutes at a fast pace to stimulate his body and mind.
2. He goes to the water fountain to *hydrate*.
3. He walks back to his office, sits down, closes his eyes, and *breathes deeply* five times.
4. He *repeats* a few affirmations as positive reinforcement, such as, "You'll be efficient, you'll make the right decisions, you'll be in the zone, and you'll attack one email at a time. Let's go!"

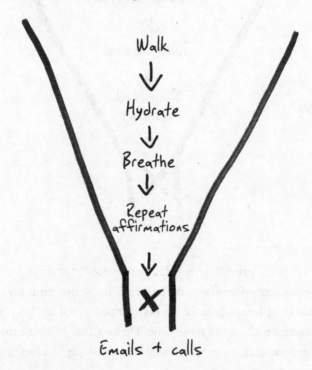

Walk
↓
Hydrate
↓
Breathe
↓
Repeat affirmations
↓
X
Emails + calls

A warm-up routine is an exceptional way of preparing for any task. If the routine is repeated on a regular basis, it becomes automatic. The brain likes to know what to expect, so at some point it associates *preparation routine* with *important task ahead*. The brain and body are then ready to cope with anticipated challenges and execute the assignment well.

You can use prep routines in all activities in which you want to see some results. Below is a description of my bedtime routine. I've been doing it for years, always in the same order, whether I'm sleeping in my bed at home or in a hotel room on the other side of the world.

1. After taking a few minutes for the usual bathroom grooming, such as flossing and brushing my teeth, I go to bed.
2. I lie down, stack two pillows under my head, and find *the* most comfortable position for reading.
3. I read for about twenty minutes.
4. When my eyelids shut despite my best efforts to stay awake, I know that I won't be able to read much longer. The second time this happens, I stop reading, slide in my bookmark, close my book, and put it on my night table.
5. I turn out the light, remove the top pillow, and place it under my right arm.
6. I roll to the left and, in less than thirty seconds, fall fast asleep. Zzzzzzz . . .

I consider sleeping an important performance. Thanks to my routine, I'm calm and free of distractions, and towards the end of it, my brain turns off instantly, like a light switch. Peaceful and restorative sleep is essential to my health and well-being, so I approach it with great respect.

Change channels

The brain sometimes operates in overdrive, with thoughts swirling in unending chaos in spite of our best efforts to calm it down. Occasionally, we also pay unreasonable and obsessive attention to a negative detail. What is the miracle cure to stop thinking irrational thoughts?

"I can't stop thinking about the mistake I just made."

"I may have received a lot of positive comments, but I can't stop thinking about the *negative* one."

"I can't be in the present moment. I'm always thinking about what will happen next."

> Sometimes, the best way to stop thinking about something is to simply think of something else.

Olympic champion Tessa Virtue told me that her preferred tactic to stop obsessing over a specific detail was to replace the thought with another one. She prefers to replace it, rather than fight it. Very savvy, Tessa!

Terry Orlick, a professor who taught me at the University of Ottawa, calls this technique *changing channels*. It's like distracting a child glued to the candy counter, looking to get her share. If the parent says, "Hey, you remember, we're going to watch a movie tonight, but we haven't picked one out yet. Which one would you like to see?" With a little luck, the thought of doing something she likes with her family will distract her from the candy. We just changed the channel!

The same strategy works for our brains. To get back to what matters and stop the obsessive thoughts, we have to focus on something else.

Train to ignore distractions

When he was just a little boy, Tiger Woods was trained with a firm hand by his father, Earl. In order to develop his son's ability to focus, Earl would distract his son at carefully chosen moments. For example, when Tiger was about to swing his club, Earl would suddenly cough or drop his golf bag. Young Tiger would, in fact, lose his concentration, become frustrated, and miss his shot.

Earl wanted to teach his son that he was master of his own thoughts and that if he became distracted by his father's cough, it's because *he chose* to be distracted. He instilled in his son the importance of focusing his attention solely on what was important: striking the ball.

This is how Tiger came to understand at a young age that a distraction only throws you off if you allow it to. As a huge Tiger fan, I'm convinced that this lesson made him one of the most dominant athletes ever. His ability to ignore all distractions at crucial moments is off the charts.

A booing crowd or a dumb mistake can only distract an athlete if they choose to let it get to them. But I have to point out that distractions are not always a nuisance as they force us to concentrate on the right things. A flashlight is a good analogy to illustrate this principle. What do I point the light at? Which details? Do I want a narrow or a broad beam of light?

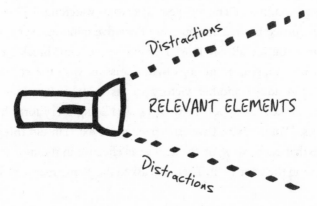

A corporate client once told me that he played blaring music for ten minutes in his office to find out which of his colleagues would be able to ignore it.

Last year, the Canadian Olympic Committee organized an event to prepare the athletes and performance staff for the 2020 Tokyo Games. During a work session, the organizers set the temperature in the room to more than 95°F to simulate the Japanese summer heat. It was a great idea to force us to stay on task while we were roasting and sweating in a small, closed room.

Take breaks

Do you know the story about the lumberjacks? You may have heard it in leadership seminars. This story illustrates the power of taking breaks.

A long time ago, lumberjack competitions were held annually in Scotland. Two lumbermen from different counties would cut long logs using an ax from early morning until late afternoon. The winner was chosen based on who had cut the most logs. That particular year, Ian, the experienced and undisputed champion, faced a young, energetic man named Garisson. The gung-ho Garisson came out strong, cutting nonstop right from the get-go and was able to pull ahead of the veteran within thirty minutes. After forty-five minutes, Ian, the older logger, stopped chopping and retreated behind a small building for fifteen minutes while Garisson continued. The villagers who were watching the event were surprised to see Ian stop every forty-five minutes, repeating the same routine all day long. Despite his frequent breaks, Ian ended up chopping more logs than Garisson, won the competition, and added another victory to his resumé. Bewildered, Garisson asked his opponent what he was doing every forty-five minutes. "Young man, I was sharpening me ax!" Ian did this to ensure that each swing of the ax was as effective in the morning as it was in the afternoon. Then, Ian asked the young man why he hadn't thought to sharpen his ax. "I didn't have time," he replied. "I had to keep choppin'."

As the saying goes, take a break before you break! If you wait until you burn out, it will already be too late. And even if you go back to the task after the break, you'll still be weakened. The same principle applies when it comes to hydration. If you only drink when you're thirsty, you're always too late. It's better to frequently drink small amounts of water to avoid becoming dehydrated.

Do you regularly take breaks? Is your brain *sharp* or *dull* in the course of your workday? When the conditions are right, people can stay focused on a task at work for about an hour. After that, the ability to focus gradually decreases.

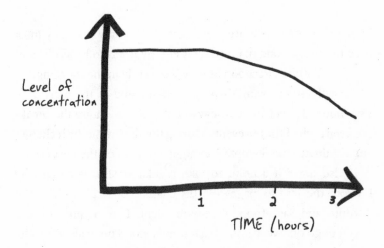

If you're like most people, you regularly monitor your phone battery to see if it needs charging, so keep an eye on yourself as well! Don't wait until your energy is too low to charge your own power.

We often pass on a break when we want to save time, especially out of fear of being judged by colleagues who might think that we are weak or lazy. Well, I would argue that people who

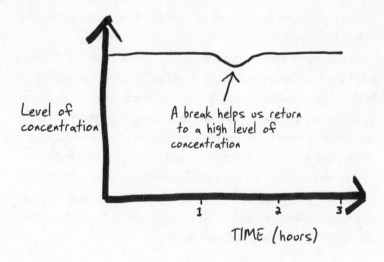

Level of
concentration

A break helps us return
to a high level of
concentration

TIME (hours)

insist on taking breaks are intelligent. They know that they must pace themselves and manage their energy levels to be as efficient at the end of the afternoon as they were early in the morning.

Decathlete Damian Warner says that some of the most decisive moments over the two days of the decathlon are the breaks between each of the ten events. During this downtime, he recharges and eliminates any disruptive thoughts to focus on the next event.

I also make it a point to take regular breaks. For example, I wrote the last six pages of this chapter on a plane between Toronto and Saskatoon, a 3.5-hour flight. I set a timer on my watch to go off every hour. Each time, I stood up, walked a little, and stretched. Obviously, these short breaks made me feel great physically, but, more importantly, they got my brain going and allowed my thoughts to take shape. In fact, most of my best ideas in this book came to me during breaks: when meditating, while drinking my latte, or during a power walk.

Think W.I.N.

I rarely talk about winning the gold medal or finishing first because, in most cases, we can't control the outcome of a competition.

There are too many external factors that can determine a result: opponents, referees, the weather, and so on.

> Thinking about winning is thinking about the outcome, and thinking about the outcome is projecting into the future.

Instead, our intention should be to control the moment. I call this principle *winning moments*. If you win several moments, you increase the likelihood of winning the competition.

Legendary football coach Lou Holtz created the acronym WIN for "what's important now" to remind his players to focus on the present moment during each game.

King of the hill Mikaël Kingsbury is incredible at putting WIN into practice. Because he's so mindful in everything he does, he keeps collecting WINs all day, every day.

- WIN moments while training in the gym
- WIN moments during mental performance coaching with JF
- WIN moments while doing interviews with journalists
- WIN moments while sitting on the chairlift
- WIN moments in the final minutes leading up to the event

He's so good at it that *winning* is now a part of his DNA. Winning is just what he does!

In the same vein, I also tell elite athletes that thinking about winning a gold medal is not practical and to focus instead on delivering a performance *worthy* of a gold medal. The nuance here is that the athlete's focus is geared towards the things they can control, like their own performance, which suddenly makes the competition less threatening. You, too, can put your focus on what's important now and create *winning moments* at the office.

- WIN moments during a meeting
- WIN moments while managing a project
- WIN moments during an important discussion
- WIN moments when fatigue starts to set in
- WIN moments during a break

By collecting these small victories, we ultimately achieve our personal goals.

Drink and eat

A study published in 2017 by Westminster and East London Universities in Britain revealed that we can increase our cognitive abilities by 25 percent thanks to . . . drinking a glass of water! We're seeing more and more people carrying their bottle of water around with them at work. Hydrating frequently is a good example to follow. Plus, more fluids in your body means more bio breaks. Extra breaks are never a bad thing!

Are you able to focus when your stomach is empty? Me neither. Athletes are highly disciplined when it comes to food intake. They're organized, they choose the best nutritional options, and they snack often. They always carry around healthy snacks in their gym bags to avoid sudden drops in energy and to respond optimally to the demands of strenuous training sessions.

Do you have healthy snacks in your handbag, backpack, or briefcase? Your brain fuels up on carbohydrates, such as whole grains, fresh or dried fruit, nuts, and green vegetables. Dark chocolate, high in cocoa, isn't a bad idea, either!

Your brain is what *drives* your performance, it's your motor, so you need to choose the right fuel for it. An efficient brain is a well-nourished brain.

Are you still *here* with me? Good. I'm *here* with you, too. Being able to focus on the right thing at the right time, on demand, is as important for workers as it is for Olympians. It's become a requirement to be efficient in our daily lives. There are a lot of distractions out there, and we must be ready to deal with them.

Be there when it counts!

CHAPTER 6

Develop an Olympian Calm

I feel like I was born to be a mental performance coach. Nothing makes me happier than to help athletes achieve their full potential. Over the years, I've helped athletes win the Super Bowl, conquer the X-Games, become world champion, and make it to the Cirque du Soleil stage. These achievements were all special, but nothing beats witnessing an athlete winning gold at the Olympic Games. Is it because they only come around every four years? Maybe. Is it because of patriotism, your country against the rest of the world? Could be. Whatever the reason, I hold the Olympic Games dear to my heart.

There are steps that an athlete must take before even thinking about winning Olympic gold. They first have to perform successfully at international competitions — World Cups and Grand Slams — and then climb onto the podium at major events, like the Pan American Games and World Championships. Similarly, an employee has to climb up the hierarchy to reach the C-suite.

When I first started working with Olympians in 2013, I had the privilege of coaching a few athletes who had already performed well on the international stage. The first major sporting event that

I attended was the Commonwealth Games in Glasgow, Scotland, in 2014. The athletes I was working with during these games podiumed, so it was mission accomplished.

My second date with major games was the Pan American Games in Toronto in 2015. I was there to coach a female wrestler who ended up dominating her opponents and capturing her first Pan Am gold medal. When she stepped on top of the podium, I was suddenly struck by the following thought: "Don't get too excited, my man. Sure, the athletes did well at the Commonwealth and the Pan Am Games, but next year is what really matters." The 2016 Rio Olympic Games were less than a year away.

That thought really hit home. I felt a mixture of fear, panic, and self-doubt. I also felt guilty for not having enjoyed the moment when the wrestler was being crowned Pan Am champion. Sitting in the stands, I was beginning to feel the pressure of the Olympic Games, even though they were still many months away. I didn't want to disappoint anyone. The athletes, the coaches, the Olympic Committee, and B2ten (an organization that hired me to work with some of Canada's top Olympians). Heck, I didn't want to disappoint myself as well!

Usually, I'm confident in my own abilities, but that evening in Toronto, I had my doubts. I experienced an overwhelming feeling that I wasn't ready for the Olympic adventure. Not to my perfectionist standards, anyways. I hated this apprehensive feeling; however, it forced me to find some answers and seek help.

When I got back home, I shared my experience with my family and closest friends. I realized that I had to become more disciplined and modify a few things in my own life. My job is to challenge athletes to get out of their comfort zone, so it dawned on me: "What about you, JF? What are you currently doing to be the best version of yourself? If the Games were held next month, would you be ready?" The answer was a resounding *no*. That's when the following mantra came to me:

If you want to work with high performers,
you need to be a high performer yourself!

I decided to get on with my mission. To my credit, I was already fit and ate healthily. I was probably tapping into 85 percent of my potential. Not bad, right? But I wanted to raise it to 95 percent. As a result, I made four changes to my life:

1. I forced myself to get the beauty sleep that I needed, regularly. I took a disciplined approach to make sleeping well at night a priority.
2. I exercised more intelligently to stimulate my metabolism. I designed a program that incorporated a series of short but intense workouts. I followed my regimen religiously, five to six times a week. My body reacted extremely well to this new training program.
3. My third challenge was changing my eating habits: smaller portion sizes, less sugar, more nuts, and less alcohol, prioritizing fresh vegetables over fruits and becoming an avid snacker to avoid hunger rages. The results were immediate. Combined with my new training regimen, I shed fifteen pounds in eight weeks. I felt amazing. When my mom first saw me after, she said, "Are you sick? You're so skinny. You need to eat more!" Oh, mother!
4. Last, I decided to manage stress better. I made an effort to eliminate many energy suckers in my life. I also meditated more. This would help free me from the small, daily stressors.

I made these changes so that my life would make more SENS: Sleep, Exercise, Nutrition, and Stress (as in stress management). It was far from being a fixer-upper, as these habits were already a part of my life. Instead, I just made sure to implement them better.

Thanks to the small tweaks, I felt an extraordinary sense of well-being, so much so that I've been religiously following this routine since 2015.

As they say, small changes can have big results.

Final preparations before Rio 2016

My sixth sense was telling me that, despite my personal improvements, I was still missing something. I took my mission seriously and really wanted to succeed. As a perfectionist, I wanted to do everything I could to face the biggest challenge of my professional career.

Of the five athletes I was coaching, three had been to the Olympics already. Given that I'd never been to the big dance, I kind of felt like an impostor working with these experienced athletes. It became clear: I had to learn more about the Olympic Games. After all, I was preparing athletes for this event, wasn't I?

But where could I find what I was searching for? It's not like there are university programs that teach how to get ready for the Olympic Games. I decided to go straight to the source. I reached out for help and managed to speak to a bunch of people who had firsthand experience in the Games.

Between September 2015 and February 2016, I interviewed twelve people: retired athletes, coaches, mental performance coaches, sport therapists, administrative support staff, and high-performance directors. I asked them to tell me, in detail, about their Olympic experiences.

They were extremely generous. Thanks to their help, I was able to put together a thirty-five-page, Olympic-sized document that I read over and over again. Here are a few important nuggets:

- You will be extremely busy, working long hours with few breaks. Take care of yourself.
- The schedule will change every day. Be prepared to adjust to any surprises, as there will be many.

- On-site, security is everywhere. As a result, it will take longer than planned to move from point A to point B. Plan your travels so that you won't have to rush.
- It will be an emotional roller coaster. Some athletes will succeed, others will fail. Expect to experience some great moments of joy and disappointment.
- The people around you will be tired and stressed out; they'll need you.
- From time to time, you'll need to get away from the frenzy of the Games to unwind. Get away from the Olympic bubble, go into town to grab dinner dressed in your normal clothes (not in national team apparel).

These tips were extremely valuable and made me feel much better prepared. My research had paid off.

During the Rio Games, I coached five athletes in four different sports: wrestling, judo, high jump, and decathlon. Two had won Olympic medals during the London Games in 2012, one was a reigning world champion, and all of them were successful internationally in their respective sports. All five athletes had a chance to podium in Rio, and the Canadian sport system had high expectations for them. But this really hit home for me after I read an article that predicted how many medals Canada was expected to win, and four out of the five athletes I coached were on the list.

Bang! A second moment of self-doubt set in.

Four months remained before the opening ceremonies. I can still see myself sitting in front of my computer, flustered by this article. I sat back in my chair, my head spinning with skeptical thoughts: "What if the athletes aren't adequately prepared? What if they perform poorly? Would it be because I let them down?"

My first reaction was to stifle the panic I felt inside. I pretended to be confident and in control, but the *fake it until you feel it* strategy wasn't enough to manage the situation. The old macho hockey coping mechanisms were resurfacing, as in "no pain, no gain!" Talk about a bad approach. My sound-sleeping nights took a hit. I was carrying extra weight on my shoulders.

After a few weeks, enough was enough, and I decided to speak out. At the time, I was a member of a mastermind group. We were six mental performance coaches who got together on monthly Skype calls to discuss our goals, share best practices, and talk about our challenges. These like-minded individuals worked in Major League Baseball, the U.S. Army, the National Football League, and other areas of elite performance. During one of our calls, I told them about the pressure I was putting on myself. They listened closely, expressed their undying support, and shared some helpful tips. I felt supported and understood.

Ten minutes later, I received an email from Bernie Holliday, the mental performance coach of the Pittsburgh Pirates.

> *Dear JF,*
>
> *Pressure is something to welcome because it means your quality preparation and successful performances have positioned you in a really cool spot to do something awesome.*
>
> *Athletes who struggle, or worse, the ones who didn't qualify for the Olympics are not going to feel any pressure in Rio because they haven't positioned themselves in a place to succeed big. They have no chance to medal!*
>
> *So, the fact that you're feeling the pressure and the fear to do right by your athletes for these upcoming Olympic Games is a testament to your great work and your success — it means you're the right guy for this!*

What do you think was my first reaction when I read this? Happy? Not at all. Satisfied? Nope.

Relieved.

I was very touched. An experienced and accomplished colleague had just confirmed that I was the man for the job. I then shrugged off the huge weight that I had been carrying around with me for weeks. I decided that the pressure weighing on me would now become my ally. It had morphed into a deep feeling of pride. I suddenly felt very privileged.

Thanks, Bernie.

I printed Bernie's email and took it with me to Rio in 2016, then PyeongChang in 2018. During the Games, the first thing I did when I woke up in the morning was reread Bernie's note. His message had such a positive impact on my career that I would like to pay it forward to you.

> *Dear Reader,*
>
> *Pressure is something to welcome because it means your quality preparation and successful performances have positioned you in a really cool spot to do something awesome.*
>
> *Struggling, or worse, disengaged workers are not going to feel any pressure because they haven't positioned themselves in a place to succeed big. They have no chance to succeed!*
>
> *So, the fact that you're feeling the pressure and the fear about future outcomes is a testament to your great work and your past success. You are an indispensable member of your organization. It means you're the right person for the job!*

Is this message relevant to you? I hope it hits the mark like it did for me.

This experience taught me some important lessons.

I had been dreaming of working with top Olympians to get

them ready for the Games . . . and there I was. *I signed up for this!* When our dreams become reality, they often carry with them the pressure to succeed. We forget that achieving our goals can generate a sense of discomfort. It's when we're in it with both feet that reality sets in. I knew, too, that many mental performance coaches would have given anything to be in my shoes.

So, in the end, feeling pressure was a privilege. I was in the enviable position of being able to fulfill my dream, which was to help others achieve *their* dreams.

The word *pressure* never gets good press. It's usually presented negatively, as in "I certainly don't want any pressure." Yet pressure isn't always a negative factor that crushes us. Over the years, I've witnessed distressing situations in which athletes collapsed under the unbearable weight that pressure can generate. But in many cases, I've seen the opposite unfold.

I address the concept of pressure almost every day in my coaching practice. Through observation and experience, I would argue that there are, in fact, two types of pressure.

The first type is the one that comes from *above*. The sort of pressure that we carry on our shoulders and weighs on us. It can paralyze you and undermine your confidence. This pressure is directly associated with negative self-talk:

- I'm afraid that I'm not good enough.
- I don't have the necessary skills.
- I only have two weeks to finish this project — I won't make it.

This type of chatter can swirl in our minds at high speeds. We then become vulnerable, and when minor setbacks arise, it typically feeds the inner turmoil and makes matters worse.

The second type of pressure is the one that comes from *behind*. It's the kick in the rear end that we sometimes need to push us forward. This inner chatter is usually constructive and realistic:

- I can't wait to attack this project! It'll be difficult, but I like the challenge.
- This exam will confirm how well I know my stuff. Let's do it!
- I'm being offered a big job, but I've been dreaming about it for a long time. I'll finally be able to use all my skills.

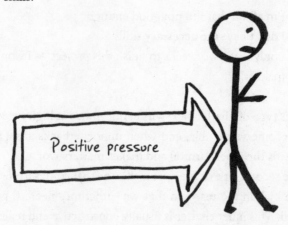

Positive pressure enables athletes to perform proactively. They're up for the challenge and are focused on what they want to achieve. It keeps them *on their toes*. Negative pressure, on the other hand, will get athletes to perform *on their heels*. They are on the defensive as their thoughts are most likely associated with what they want to avoid.

Before we go any further, there's a basic principle that we need to address about the pressure we feel: it's a matter of perspective.

Pressure is not a situation, a person, a context, or an environment. Pressure is simply something we feel that is entirely constructed by our own minds. *We* are the source of the pressure.

I remember my hockey defense partner would fall apart when we played in front of large crowds. The poor guy, his nervousness would take over, and his performance suffered for it. In contrast, I usually played my best games when the stands were jam-packed.

Olympians post their best results during the most stressful moments. Ask Olympic champions how they felt just before their performance, they'll tell you that it was the most stressful moment of their lives . . . and they won gold! Therefore, intense moments of pressure can also be beneficial, right? You must refuse to let the pressure rule over you and instead make it your ally.

Pressure also comes from below to make you go higher

Canadian high jumper Derek Drouin knows all about dealing with pressure. In preparation for Rio 2016, he boasted some impressive results and entered the Olympic year firing on all cylinders. Already a bronze medalist at the 2012 London Olympics, he added several victories to his repertoire, including Pan American and World Championship gold medals in 2015. Most of Derek's competitors saw him as the man to beat in Rio. His sport federation and coaches were also confident that he was a serious medal contender: expectations were high. Third in London was great, but Derek knew that Rio was the perfect time to peak. He had to turn this pressure to his advantage and make it come from behind to realize his childhood dream.

Derek started his 2016 season like any other, slowly but surely. His fitness level evolved through steady, well-orchestrated improvements. Everything was happening as planned.

In April 2016, four months before the Games, Derek was suffering from persistent back trouble. Small aches and pains that require minimal care are normal, but he knew that this was different. The medical team conducted a series of tests, including an MRI. The results revealed horrible news: two lumbar vertebrae showed small fractures.

Derek found out he had a broken back four months before the most important moment of his life.

Can you imagine receiving shocking news like this? All sorts of emotions surfaced: anxiety mixed with anger, frustration, and concern. Clearly, the plan leading up to the Games had to change.

Two possibilities lay before him: he could embark on a specialized physical conditioning program to strengthen his lower back and hope that it would make it until the Games, or he could take five weeks off to allow the fractures to heal and still have ten weeks to pick up where he had left off.

It was a risky bet, but he chose the second option. Do you have any idea how hard it is for an athlete to step away from their sport, let alone a few months before the Olympics? Well, let me tell you, there's nothing worse for an athlete than forced inactivity. They're so invested in their sport, not being able to do it affects their identity and self-esteem. The same can be said for workers who are highly engaged in their careers.

Despite the uncertainty, Derek's behavior was outstanding. He followed the medical team's instructions to a T. He didn't rush things. Even if he couldn't train physically, he could still train his mind. He *sensalized* daily and slept long hours; Netflix became his best friend!

After five weeks, Derek felt substantially less pain. The prognosis seemed encouraging, and Derek was ready to begin training again.

As a precautionary measure, and for his own peace of mind, he decided to have another MRI to get an update.

The results showed that the fractures were still there, with minimal improvement.

I sensed that Derek was frustrated, and rightfully so. The danger was refusing to accept the situation and becoming bogged down in pondering *Why me, why now? This is unfair.* The temptation was strong to see the last five weeks as a complete waste of time.

The reality was that he was running out of time. The priority now was to look at the situation objectively, not subjectively. It's much more constructive to deal *with* a situation than stubbornly fight *against* it.

> It is what it is, not what it's supposed to be.

To become an Olympic champion, Derek had to jump close to 2.4 meters, or nearly eight feet. That's the height of a standard ceiling in a house. With ten weeks left, Derek's support team understood that it would be tight. I asked him if he still believed he could win gold. Given his highly competitive nature, I was expecting a resounding *yes!* Instead, he said, "I don't know because I've never had to prepare for the Olympic Games with a broken back."

He was right.

It was much too early to think about the outcome of his event. To bring the conversation back on track, I then asked him if he thought he could get better by the end of the week. He thought so. From that moment on, the plan was to prepare for Rio with small short-term goals. The motto became, "Get better every week."

Derek had five competitions leading up to the Olympics. He was able to jump 2.2 meters during the first event of the series. It was a far cry from the required 2.4 meters, but Derek remained realistic, reminding himself that, "It is what it is, not what it's supposed to be. One week at a time." His sole objective became to do a little better next time.

Kudos to Derek's medical team and his jumping coach, Jeff Huntoon. They were instrumental in helping Derek improve his marks a few centimeters at a time despite the pain caused by his back. The fifth and final competition was held in Eberstadt, Germany, three weeks before the Games. Derek blew us all away with a 2.38-meter jump! At that precise moment, he *knew* that he could win Olympic gold in Rio.

Let's fast-forward to the Games.

Rio de Janeiro, August 14, 2016. Derek posted a 2.29-meter jump to qualify for finals. Two days later, on a hot and humid evening, the 6-foot-4 Canadian stood in the enormous 78,000-seat stadium, preparing for the high jump finals. I sat in the first row with the other members of Derek's support team, including members of B2ten. We were following every step of the way as Derek started at 2.20 meters, then 2.25m . . . 2.29m . . . 2.33m . . . 2.36m. The competitors are eliminated after three consecutive missed attempts, and at this point, most of Derek's rivals had already thrown in the towel except for the Ukrainian and Qatari jumpers.

The bar was raised to 2.38 meters, with Derek scheduled to jump first. He knew it was doable as he had done it in Germany a few weeks earlier. From our vantage point, we watched him closely as he performed his pre-jump routine. Focused face, confident posture, deep breaths. We could sense that he was in his zone, experiencing this moment of intense pressure with true Olympian calm.

He was eyeing the bar like a lion stares at his prey: *I've got this.* Just before he started his approach, he simulated the jumping motions one last time to feel it throughout his body. Starting with a hop, he began his approach. In just a few strides, he arrived at the bar, planted his foot, and propelled his body through the air. He grazed the bar, but it held.

Derek cleared 2.38 meters!

We were ecstatic! His two opponents were now under huge pressure from above. Eventually, they both failed to clear the bar, and Derek was crowned champion.

That's right, folks. Derek Drouin won Olympic gold with a broken back.

I jumped with joy and celebrated the moment with Dominick Gauthier and JD Miller, the founders of B2ten. Then I broke down in tears. Derek had accomplished his lifelong dream despite all the setbacks. His performance left me stunned. It was the first time as a mental performance coach that an athlete I was coaching had won gold at the Olympics.

That evening in Rio, all of us hugged each other and cried tears of joy together. What a moment! Grown adults, openly and genuinely showing their emotions. Almost seems strange, doesn't it? You should try it at work. It's an excellent way to create team chemistry.

I will be forever in awe of Derek's achievement. He demonstrated such poise, resiliency, and maturity throughout the entire process. All of this in the face of extreme adversity and with the stakes so high. What an athlete!

I experienced an aha moment in Brazil. Living this journey with Derek right up to the gold medal confirmed that I was in the right field. I also realized how privileged I was to experience the pressure that comes with helping Olympians achieve their dreams.

Looking back, I recognize that Derek helped *me* go further. His extraordinary accomplishment under such difficult circumstances taught me four important lessons. I would like to share them with you so that you, too, are better equipped to deal with pressure.

Focus on short-term goals

Paying too much attention to a long-term goal can cause anxiety. It's hard to get a real handle on the way things will evolve when we're fixed on a deadline that is months away. Furthermore, things rarely if ever unfold exactly the way we imagined them anyway, so what use is it to be so obsessed with the future so far ahead? Keeping your focus short term, taking things one week at a time, can be reassuring. "What do I need to do in the next six days?" is far less distressing than "What do I need to in the next six months?" The *next few days* are within our reach, so the burden becomes lighter, and the tasks that need to be done are easier to handle. Short-term goals also help us acknowledge and celebrate the small victories to feed our fire. The get-better-ev-ery-week approach enabled Derek to focus on small gains, avoid discouragement, and stay away from the uncertainties associated with being able to compete or not in Brazil.

In the corporate world, executives often attach too much importance to quarterly and mid-year targets. Don't get me wrong, medium- and long-term goals are important, but if you obsess about them all the time, how attentive are you to taking care of your daily business?

Whatever the challenge may be, you can get there, *one week at a time*.

Remember, it is what it is, and not what it's supposed to be

Derek couldn't ask the International Olympic Committee to postpone the Games for a few months because of his back injury. Qualifications were scheduled for August 14, and the final for August 16. Period.

People who are mentally tough have this ability to see things as they really are, whether good or bad, and just deal with them. Typically, we complain about situations when we don't want to be challenged. The problem is that this negative mental framework prevents us from seeing the solutions and moving forward. Remember that it's always easier to deal with a situation than to fight against it.

For example, you're initially asked to produce a report within the week, but then your boss changes their mind and now wants it done within three days. Instinctively, you may get upset when thinking about the shorter deadline. But when there's nothing you can do about it, what use is it to get overly worked up about the situation? It's much more efficient to shift your outlook and adapt to the new reality.

Derek demonstrated that we can still achieve an exceptional goal, even in a very complicated situation. I often tell my clients, "Find a way to be amazing in crappy conditions."

Accept pressure in your life

When I think back to Derek's gold medal, it seems to me that his injury had a positive impact, not a negative one.

His injured back forced him to focus on only the basic elements to train efficiently. His preparation plan was reduced considerably, leaving him with no wiggle room to coast along without being purposeful. His back was against the wall. He had no choice but to be perfect every day in training. The pressure that Derek felt to be ready for the Games imposed robust self-discipline. Healthy pressure can make us superefficient, even when we're highly vulnerable.

Take a few minutes to think about some pressure that you've experienced at the office.

- Do you see this pressure negatively or as a way to make you better?
- Do you use this pressure to improve your self-discipline?
- Does this pressure bring you back to the basics to ensure that you're getting things done right?

My friends at Cirque du Soleil who are responsible for creating new shows feel enormous pressure in the months leading up to each premiere. When the tickets are sold out, you can't waste any time. You must meet the deadline. In the home stretch, they work twelve to fourteen hours a day, six days a week. The show must go on! In retrospect, they recognize that they're able to produce exceptional shows thanks to the pressure they feel leading up to the premiere. A veteran Cirque du Soleil choreographer was telling me that having too much time wasn't necessarily better, because there was always the danger of becoming complacent and lazy.

If Derek had magically been allocated a few extra months to prepare for the Games, would he have achieved the same outcome in Rio? We will never know. But one thing's for sure, he beat his own path to gold by maximizing the time *he did have*.

Maintain your goal even if the route changes

At work as in sports, there is always more than one way to reach the ultimate goal. Having an alternative plan is always helpful. If plan A is no longer working, we move on to plan B. It's reassuring to know that there are other solutions.

Think of a situation in which you felt stuck at work. Things were not going as you had anticipated, and you're racked with doubt.

Was it difficult for you to look at the situation differently? Were you able to come up with the right plan B? Would you approach this situation the same way were you to confront it again?

One of my close friends is a successful attorney specializing in corporate law. He uses a technique that he calls "answers in my back pocket." When he's getting ready to meet a client, he strategically anticipates all the questions likely to come up so that he's never caught off guard. He also foresees all avenues that the negotiations could potentially take so that he can show up at the meeting with multiple solutions in his back pocket. I've rarely witnessed someone who comes up with answers to problems the way he can. His tag line is, "If options A, B, and C don't work, no sweat. The alphabet has twenty-six letters."

In Derek's case, he was forced to take a totally different tack heading into the Games. He had to completely remodel the plan: the number of jumping sessions, the competition schedule, the training loads, and the recovery breaks. He had never prepared this way for a major competition. He had to let go of plan A and turn to plan B, which worked out perfectly for him in Rio.

Let's define stress

I believe that the word "stress" is not always used correctly. Too many people use it as a generalized term to describe most of the negative emotions that we experience.

Stress is simply a reaction that our body experiences from dealing with a stimulus. In other words, when we go through any kind of change, we are stressed. The famous researcher Hans Selye determined that there is good stress (*eustress*) and bad stress (*distress*). The first relates to emotions such as joy, excitement, and enthusiasm, while the second refers to anxiety, frustration, and exhaustion.

We may look at stress negatively, but we actually need it to grow and excel. For example, the entire fundamental principle of sports training is based on inducing specific amounts of stress in the mind and the body to make them more powerful. Without these reactions to stress, they can't respond to increasingly demanding challenges.

As a matter of fact, few people experience radically stressful variations as often as elite athletes do. They can be in full *eustress* when they win championships and in deep *distress* when performing less well than expected.

The effects of stress on our bodies is similar to the variations on an electrocardiogram. It's better to see the ups and downs rather than a flat line, right? When a client arrives in my office and tells me they're stressed, I say, "Great! That means you're alive."

The point is, stress doesn't mean *negative*. An ecstatic moment of joy can be just as stressful on the body as an episode of intense frustration.

Make your butterflies fly in formation

Congratulations! You've just been asked to speak before a room full of people, the one thing that really makes you nervous. Just thinking about it makes you feel woozy. When the time comes, your heart is pounding, your palms are sweating, and you're looking for the exit.

Because you dread these types of situations, you're not in tune with the moment.

Nervousness is actually a good thing to experience. Put simply, it's a natural mechanism that our brain triggers so that we can respond to an important challenge. We become nervous because the challenge means something, because we care. When was the last time you were nervous about something that you were indifferent about? Without nervousness, we wouldn't be able to achieve our full potential.

A typical symptom that we feel is butterflies in our gut. Do you know what causes them? When the brain detects a threatening situation, it releases adrenalin, which can temporarily harm the digestive system. Blood leaves the areas where it's not needed, such as the stomach, and flows towards other areas of the body, like our muscles, that are called upon to do more. Butterflies are small contractions caused by a lack of oxygen in the blood, so less blood in the stomach = less oxygen = butterflies. That's all it is.

> The problem isn't the nervousness. On the contrary. Nervousness helps us prepare. Becoming nervous *because we're nervous* is the problem!

Once again, it's important to have the right attitude.

In the end, having butterflies is not bad, unless you decide it is. When Mikaël Kingsbury stood at the top of the course before his gold medal run at the Olympics, he had a whole army of butterflies in his stomach! Four years had passed since his second-place finish at the Sochi Games, and he was looking for revenge. This moment meant the world to him. We knew ahead of time that the butterflies would also travel to South Korea, but Mik wasn't worried at all. He had a plan to work with — not against — the situation. When the butterflies finally showed up, instead of "Oh, shit!" buzzing in his mind, it was "Oh, yes!" One word can make all the difference.

Butterflies will always be there in times of major stress. After all, we're humans, not robots. We just have to make sure that our butterflies fly in formation.

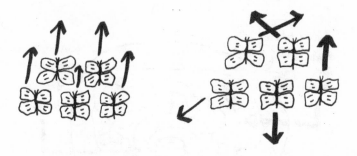

Butterflies heading in the same direction means having the ability to feel comfortable with the uncomfortable. This works while performing for a global audience, going through a job interview, or writing a test at school.

The impulsive brain

To explain how the brain operates in moments of high stress, we often refer to the example of a primitive human being who encounters a bear. The cognitive response to this threatening meeting is managed by the limbic system, also called the emotional brain. The primary function of this section of the brain is to ensure survival. It acts on impulse to protect us.

The involuntary reaction, commonly referred to as the *fight-or-flight response*, may be practical to protect ourselves from dangerous encounters, but it's not very useful at work. When you have an impulsive reaction that you regret five minutes later, wondering *Why did I say that?*, know that your limbic system is to blame.

The prefrontal cortex, also called the smart brain, is the part of the brain that you want to prioritize at work. Located in the frontal lobe, it helps capture and analyze information to produce a desired response. The prefrontal cortex is responsible for great performances on the field and in the workplace, especially when there are stressful distractions everywhere. We'll come back to this point later on.

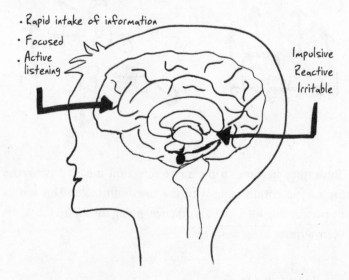

Let's get back to the emotional brain. Our limbic system is also responsible for generating the emotion of fear. In my work, I hear stories of fear every day:

- fear of disappointing
- fear of the unknown
- fear of not being up to snuff
- fear of risk
- fear of not being liked
- fear of failure
- fear of losing
- fear of getting injured

What is a fear? Does it really exist?

Fear is nothing more than a story we tell ourselves. Since it refers to a future event, there's nothing that guarantees that it will actually happen. Yet we still convince ourselves to believe our fears. In the end, it's only as intense as we make it.

Since our limbic system protects us against potential danger, we have a natural tendency to exaggerate the threat. The more we feed it, the more it scares us. However, after going through a daunting situation, we often realize that it wasn't as terrifying as we had thought it would be.

In the end, it wasn't that bad.

This means that the made-up story was worse than the actual situation. Think about the wasted time and energy! Based on experience, I would argue that approximately 80 percent of our fears never happen or, at least, not as we had imagined them.

Keep in mind the popular acronym FEAR: false evidence appearing real. It's a simple way of remembering that most fears aren't true and are often nothing more than a story that we've invented in our own minds.

Like nervousness, fear can also be our ally. Being afraid forces us to focus our attention on the basic elements to achieve our goals. If you're scared to flunk your exam, you'll modify your schedule to study more, right?

Canadian figure skater Tessa Virtue had her own acronym for the Olympic Games in South Korea. Remembering that FEAR could also serve as a launching pad, she loved this version: Face Everything And Rise. She wanted to attack the Games, not become a victim of them.

> To better control your fears, ask yourself,
> "Do I need to be this scared?" Usually the answer is *no*.
> This simple question helps normalize the situation
> so that we can see it differently.

Once again, perspective is key. The way we manage fear determines its impact on our behavior.

Stop caring and let go!

I've noticed that one of the most common fears in the workplace is the worry of being judged by others.

- Does my boss think highly of me?
- Does the client appreciate my services?
- What do my colleagues think of me?

Learn to ignore it. Your time is way too precious! Besides, very few individuals will tell you what they really think about you. You don't believe me? How many times have you told a colleague what you really think of them? Exactly.

As a keynote speaker, if I worried about what everybody thought of me, I wouldn't sleep anymore! The truth is, we'll never satisfy everyone, even if we try.

During a business trip, I met a speaker whose area of expertise is *human happiness*. She mentioned that what differentiates happy people is their tendency to let go more than their less happy counterparts do. In other words, stop caring so much, especially on issues that are out of your control.

Olympians are criticized all the time by judges, opponents, coaches, the media, and fans. They become very skilled at brushing off nasty comments or, at least, at taking them with a grain of salt. Sometimes, they just don't care. They choose to remain focused on what they can control.

Do you worry too much? Do you wonder what other people say about you?

If you do, sometimes the most efficient method is to simply not give a damn! Don't get me wrong, it's important to respect others, but, for the good of your mental health, letting go of useless comments is highly beneficial. This strategy can help you deal with office gossipers, trying competitors, or social media critics.

Adjust your thermostat

Peter Jensen is a successful mental performance coach who has contributed to a number of great Canadian triumphs over the years. Known for his creative methods, he uses a thermostat as a metaphor to illustrate the ability to remain cool when the pressure's on.

In our homes, we set the thermostat to a desired temperature, such as 72°F. The thermostat will then take into account the ambient variations and readjust to maintain a constant temperature. It dictates what the temperature will be. On the other hand, a thermometer doesn't have the same adaptive system. It simply measures and indicates the temperature in a room but has no influence over it.

> Elite performers manage themselves like thermostats:
> they stay cool when the heat is on.

To manage pressure better during competitions, one of the coaches I know wears a smart watch with a heart rate monitor to track his physiological state. As it is, he's known as a leader who is constantly in control of his emotions and always says the right things at the right time.

We have to know ourselves well to self-regulate like a thermostat. Elite athletes spend so much time training their bodies, they intuitively develop amazing self-awareness. Their bodies send constant feedback to the brain indicating whether the drill is challenging, easy, tiring, comfortable, and so on. Subsequently, athletes understand what causes symptoms, such as:

- sweaty palms,
- dry mouth,
- stuttering voice,
- additional muscle tension; and
- quick heart rate.

To perform well, athletes must first know their optimal activation level. They can't be too relaxed, but they can't be too hyped up either. Have you ever heard the saying *never too high, never too low*? Think about guitar strings. To produce a perfect sound, they can't be too tight or too loose. The same thing applies to human performance.

To help performers find a happy medium, I use a scale of 1 to 10. The number 1 signifies a state of deep relaxation, and 10 represents an excessive emotional state with little self-control. The first step is to determine the number that indicates the *ideal level* of activation. For a hockey player, this number could be 7; for a golfer, 5; and for a boxer, 8. Next, we describe what this number means. For example, when a tennis player is at 7, this means that:

- they're relaxed physically,

- they're maintaining a positive inner chatter
- they're feeling confident; and
- they're breathing well.

Numbers 5, 6, 8, and 9 are also defined to help the athlete understand what is too low and too high. Thanks to specific self-regulation techniques, the athlete is able to tone it down or turn it up to get back to their sweet spot, just like the thermostat that readjusts to come back to the desired temperature.

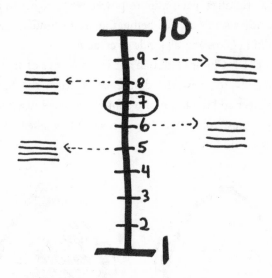

If you're looking to better self-regulate, this scale is simple, concrete, and easy to use.

Activate your thermostat.

Fill your toolbox

There are plenty of ways to manage stressors to help us tap into our Olympian calm. To finish off the chapter, I will share a few of my go-to techniques. Hopefully some of them will serve you well.

Walking

We often forget that walking is the most effective and natural form of exercise there is. It doesn't require a gym membership, a fancy piece of equipment, or a teammate to rely on. All it takes is a pair of comfortable shoes. It's not the most strenuous workout, but it still produces endorphins, our brain's favorite anti-stress hormone.

I regularly walk in my neighborhood on workdays. These short breaks always do me good. I mean, when's the last time you felt awful after a ten-minute power walk, right? In addition to producing a sense of well-being, the brain stimulation you get from walking generates all kinds of creative ideas.

In 2009, Dr. Charles Hillman at the University of Illinois used brain imaging to show the difference between the brain of a seated subject and the brain of a subject who had just walked for twenty minutes. You can see the areas of the walker's brain that are fully activated.

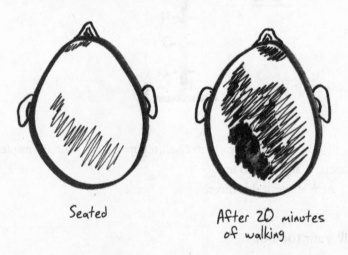

Seated

After 20 minutes of walking

A client of mine who is a corporate leader for a beverage company will take a brisk walk when he feels his temper starting to rise. He refuses to be controlled by his limbic system! His five-minute power walk is enough to free his mind so that he can respond properly to the situation that provoked his anger. Now that's a corporate Olympian!

Breathe like an Olympian

We breathe without being aware of it. It's an automated process. But if we want to use our breath to calm ourselves down, we need to focus on it. Conscious breathing is a skill, and, like any skill, it needs to be trained if we want to use it properly. It gets rid of muscle tension and it diminishes neurological activity, but, more importantly, breathing has the ability to connect us to the present moment.

Do you practice conscious breathing? If you do, great. When I ask this question during a talk, very few people raise their hands. The most common excuse? They don't have the time.

Conscious breathing (also called mindful breathing) is regularly associated with meditation practices such as being attentive to your breath for five, ten, or even twenty minutes. But you don't need much more than a couple of minutes to benefit from it. Athletes learn to briefly concentrate on their breathing several times a day so that they can flush their minds and refocus on the task at hand.

Below is a simple-to-use breathing exercise that you can implement at work. All you need to do is find a comfortable spot in a quiet place and follow these three steps:

1. Take ten deep breaths by taking three to four seconds to inhale and five to six seconds to exhale. Longer exhalation triggers the relaxation effect. If you need to activate yourself, do the opposite. When you exhale quickly, you increase your activation level. For those reasons, breathing is an excellent way to find your sweet spot on your activation scale.
2. Inhale through the nose and exhale through the mouth (or the nose, if you prefer). It's important to inhale through the nose, as its filtration system purifies the air before it reaches the lungs.

3. While inhaling, expand the chest first, then the abdomen. When exhaling, deflate the abdomen first, then the chest.

Two minutes once a day is all it takes to notice some benefits. After a few weeks, you'll start having more control over impulsive thoughts associated with stressful situations. If you are new to mindful breathing, there are some simple guided-breathing apps, such as Breathe Easy, to help you get started.

Breathing is free, and you can do it whenever and wherever you want. Use it!

Don't be perfect, be excellent!

In his biography, former National Hockey League superstar Bobby Orr explained that he used to break down his seventy-game season into seven blocks of ten games. He understood that having short-term goals was smart. In each of these blocks, his objective was to play well during eight games out of ten, keeping some leeway for the lousy games that every player experiences once in a while. This method eliminated the pressure to be perfect. Instead, Bobby chose to work towards excellence.

Having a perfection mindset is a double-edged sword. It pushes us to set ambitious goals, but the risks of disappointment and discouragement are high. When perfectionist athletes don't perform well, they experience agony and frustration, while extreme perfectionists feel anger, even rage.

I encourage them instead to develop an excellence mentality. Excellence doesn't mean succeeding 100 percent of the time, but almost.

When you compare the two mindsets, it's fascinating to see how different they are. Together with an elite athlete, I developed this comparative table, which has become a useful memory aid to help him prepare for a competition.

Perfectionist Mentality	Excellence Mentality
100%	85–99%
I will nail every element	I will nail most elements
Unrealistic	Realistic
Failure is inevitable	Success is possible
Mistakes are unacceptable	Mistakes are expected
Has difficulty adapting	Easily adapts
Unachievable results	Results are achievable thanks to a plan
Controlling	Spontaneous
Gives up	Perseveres

As you can see, the excellence mentality allows for mistakes to be made and generates far less negative pressure. It deals with reality, not fantasy.

Let's take a multiple-choice exam as an example. The perfectionist believes they know everything. They start the exam in full force. Then, they arrive at question 10, which they can't answer, and they start panicking. They struggle to proceed to the subsequent questions because they keep thinking about question 10. On the other hand, students with an excellence mindset walk into class telling themselves *they know a lot* about the subject. When they get to question 10, they remain calm and move on to the next question, as they understand that excellence is still possible, even if they answer this question incorrectly.

Take a step back

If I asked you to stand with your nose pressed against the wall and to tell me what you see, you wouldn't be able to tell me much more than the paint color, right? Now, if I asked you to take a big step back, you would see the picture frame on the left and the window moulding on the right.

When a client says to me, "I can't stop thinking about *x*," I make them stand up, press their face against the wall for one to two minutes, and describe how they feel and what they see. Then I make them take a step back. Usually, those who go along quickly learn the lesson: without perspective, we don't see much.

In a problematic situation, taking a step back helps us see things more clearly. If an issue keeps spinning around in our minds and monopolizes our thoughts, we're not able to grasp the answers.

Sometimes, all you need to do is to step away and come back to the issue later. The old cliché *sleep on it* is a great example. Delaying making an important decision until the following day allows for more time to consider it and even to generate some new ideas.

I said it earlier — it's not the problem that's the problem, it's the way we look at it. So, take a step back!

Find the right words

We need to be careful about the words we choose to describe how we're feeling. When we use the word *stressed* to describe our current state, we're generalizing our emotion instead of indicating exactly what it is that we're experiencing.

Are we feeling frustration, exasperation, nervousness, or fear?

Despite apparent similarities, there are important subtleties that distinguish our emotions. By using the right word, the one that describes exactly what we're feeling, it becomes easier to find solutions.

When I help a client accurately define what they're feeling, I notice that they're somewhat relieved. "Yes, that's exactly it!" It's always easier to unravel a negative emotion when we're able to put our finger on it.

An Olympian had this bad habit of referring to all unpleasant situations as *problems*. I made him realize that this word got his limbic system firing, probably more than he wanted. Since he is a perfectionist, it created additional unnecessary pressure that weighed heavily on his mind. Together, we decided that words like *challenge* and *situation* would be easier to handle. These words were far less threatening and enabled him to behave more calmly. With them, he had switched to the smart brain, the prefrontal cortex.

Sometimes, we need someone else

There are times when we feel stuck. We just don't know how to respond to the challenging situation ahead of us. Caught off guard, we scramble to find answers. The tool that we can't find in our own box may be in someone else's. All we have to do is ask ourselves what this trusted person would do in this situation, and we may just hit the nail on the head.

Judoka Antoine Valois-Fortier uses this strategy every so often. He's mentioned to me that Nicolas Gill (his judo mentor), Scott Livingston (his strength and conditioning coach), and I were three coaches that always gave him sound advice. If he runs out of ideas to manage a stressful moment, he asks himself, "What would they tell me right now?"

Who is this person for you, the one who always seems to offer the proper guidance?

Avoid dramatizing

When things don't go as expected, high achievers tend to dramatize and exaggerate. For example, many hockey players place way too much emphasis on the oh-so-important first shift of the game: "My first shift wasn't good. I won't have a good game today." I knew a volleyball player who had a similar mentality. If she made a few bad bumps early in the game, her brain would jump to conclusions such as, "I just don't have it in me today."

What about you? Do you dramatize and jump to conclusions when you struggle early in your workday? "I'm off today!" or "Oh boy, I'm in for the long haul!"

> A bad morning doesn't equal a bad day.
> A bad day doesn't equal a bad week.
> And failing doesn't mean that you're a failure.

Besides, you really don't need to add fuel to the fire considering your limbic system already dramatizes instinctively, right?

"?" or "!"

I was in a treatment room with an Olympian and the athletic therapist at the PyeongChang Games. It was the day before the competition. We were talking about everything under the sun while the athlete was getting treated. All of a sudden, I noticed that the athlete was no longer participating in the conversation.

"Cat got your tongue?" I asked.

"Yeah, sorry," they said. "I'm asking myself a lot of questions right now."

"Are you answering them?" I quickly replied, grinning slightly.

The athlete looked me right in the eye and said, "Heck no! That's why I'm so mixed up!"

Questioning is generally synonymous with feeling uncertain and worried. I explained to the athlete that questioning ourselves (?) in pressure moments is normal, but we have to offer our brains convincing answers (!) to turn the inner interrogation around.

The next day, after having warmed up for the event, the Olympian came over to me and said, "Hey JF, I've got a lot of answers today. I'm going to nail my performance!"

Inner chatter ending with question marks leads to self-doubt. Constructive affirmations ending with exclamation points lead to self-assurance.

Does your self-talk have more "?" or more "!"? If your brain is throwing questions at you, make sure you give it the answers it deserves. Otherwise, your mind will get caught up in assumptions, doubts, and worries.

The CRAP method

A professional hockey player had trouble controlling his emotions on the bench after a bad shift. He kept using the word *crap* to describe his performance. "That shift was crap!" His words, not mine!

The player needed a specific guideline to manage himself on the bench. To make the technique catchy, I used my creative thinking and came up with *crap* as an acronym. *C* was for *calm*. Taking deep breaths would help him ease the inner turmoil before moving on to the second step, *R* for *reflection*. Once he was calm, he would be able to reason objectively, see the situation as it was, and understand why the mistakes happened. "I rushed the play and made a blind pass. That explains the giveaway." Next came *A* for *adjustment*, replacing the mistake with a solution using sensalization: *Take a second to look up before making the pass.* The last letter, *P*, was for *preparation*. This step would make him go back to the important reminders that he had set for himself before the game.

Calm

Reflection

Adjustment

Preparation

The Olympian at work has to find ways to manage overwhelming stress. We often have to face the unexpected, just like athletes do on the playing field. To respond appropriately, we must calm our minds to tackle challenges effectively.

In the next, final chapter, we'll address topics like perseverance, grit, courage, and determination.

With just one chapter to go, we're almost at the finish line. Don't stop now!

CHAPTER 7

Put Some *Sisu* into It

When I worked at Cirque du Soleil, one of my duties was to facilitate workshops on various mental training skills and concepts. One of these workshops focused on perseverance.

Fifteen new circus performers from across the globe had just arrived in Montreal, where Cirque's international headquarters are located. These artists were in town to begin their specialized training programs before joining different touring shows around the world. In addition to learning complex acrobatic tricks, the new arrivals also took artistic classes to learn how to dance, sing, apply makeup, and act like clowns. Sounds fun, doesn't it? But I can tell you that these training programs are far from being a walk in the park. They are difficult and extremely exhausting. Plus, some of them were about to join shows that performed 475 times a year. Needless to say, the topic of perseverance was on point for the entire group.

A Finnish artist came up to me after the workshop. With an energetic tone of voice, he explained that back home, the concepts of perseverance and resilience are called *sisu* ("see-zoo"). This Finnish word is a philosophy of life taught to all children as early as preschool. Families live by it and pass it on from generation to generation as if it were a national treasure.

Sisu is difficult to translate. There isn't one English word that can perfectly incorporate all the nuances of this Finnish principle. The artist told me that the word *perseverance* comes close, but *sisu* also implies grit, courage, tenacity, and resilience . . . multiplied by ten! I'm fascinated by the power of words and I had never heard this term before, so I was curious to know more. "You know, JF, when you must face an enormous challenge and you've given it your all, you've used up all of your mental stamina and you feel the time has come to let go before you collapse?" I grinned and nodded. He continued: "Well, when you've reached the point where you're about to throw in the towel, that's the moment when *sisu* comes into play." I understood that *sisu* is the ability to go beyond our limits, not just to persevere.

I was so intrigued; I couldn't get enough.

The young Finn explained that winning a gold medal or coming in first isn't the ultimate goal in Finland. The real victory is never, ever giving up, regardless of the circumstances. "If you can look at yourself in the mirror and honestly say that you pushed yourself to the limit, that you couldn't go any further, you're a winner. For our people, the only significant victory is the mental victory. Since I was a young child, I've been told repeatedly that if I win the mental battles, I'll be a winner in life. I made it to Cirque du Soleil thanks to the *sisu* philosophy."

Our conversation was a real eye-opener. Astonished, I wanted to know everything about this patriotic Suomi mental principle. I read a whole host of historical facts about Finns for whom *sisu* had changed the course of their lives. I also came across stories about the war against the Russians and other nationalistic exploits that marked the Finnish culture.

During my Google searches, I also came across a well-known name in the sports world: the former captain of the Montreal

Canadiens, Finland's own Saku Koivu. Saku embodies the meaning of *sisu*. Small in size, he had a stellar career at a time when bigger players dominated the NHL. In 2001, the hockey nation was shocked when Koivu announced that he was suffering from intra-abdominal non-Hodgkin's lymphoma. Gritty as ever, he kept a positive attitude and fought for his life. His perseverance prevailed, and he finally won the battle against cancer. Hockey fans remember the emotional moment on April 9, 2002, when number 11 came back after missing seventy-nine regular season games. As soon as he hopped onto the ice, the crowd gave him a nine-minute standing ovation. It was a really special moment in sporting history, and *sisu* played a major role in it.

People who adhere to *sisu* don't go unnoticed. There's an aura about them. These individuals just never quit. They always look to bounce back after being knocked down. We despise them when they're opponents; we love them as teammates. They are fierce competitors, yet kind towards others and concerned about their well-being. What employer wouldn't want an employee like this?

Develop your *sisu*

In my line of work, I get to cross paths with performers who have demonstrated *sisu* under unusual circumstances. You'll read about some of their stories later on. I'll also share some easy-to-use strategies to help develop your own *sisu*. I use the word *develop* because every one of us has *sisu* in our gut. As a matter of fact, you were one heck of a go-getter in the first few months of your life without realizing it.

One of the first major challenges we face as human beings is learning to walk. Just take a second to think about it: walking is no easy feat. Have you ever noticed the number of attempts a baby makes before they can finally walk?

Long before they're able to take a few steps, babies must go through preliminary checkpoints. A rigorous process that lasts several months awaits them: the baby learns to balance itself while sitting, then discovers crawling, followed by moving on all fours, then standing up while holding on to a piece of furniture. The baby falls over and over again before the hard work finally pays off, that miraculous day when it takes a few steps before falling into its parents' arms. Respect!

Babies never get discouraged. They may express their frustration at times, but they will not give up. Tenacious, they will persevere in the face of failure until they can take that first step. In their little minds, they know they will succeed. It's not a question of if, but when. An amazing display of *sisu*! We adults could learn a few things from these little creatures. Our powerful adult minds can hold us back by endlessly overthinking and shying away from risks.

If an adult had to learn how to walk, knowing how difficult that task is, would they be gritty enough to successfully conquer every arduous checkpoint along the way?

How many times have you refused to take on a new challenge because it required an additional effort? Do you lose the mental battle before even taking up a difficult task?

Olympians and babies: same breed

Earlier in the book, we discussed the lifestyle of Olympians. Their lives are fairly simple and structured to the smallest detail. They don't have a lot of responsibilities other than those that concern their sport. But a simple life doesn't mean an easy life. There are few occupations (playing a sport is a profession, even if we still refer to Olympians as "amateur athletes") that require pushing the physical and mental boundaries, day after day, the way elite athletes do.

If an athlete aspires to become a world champion one day, they must accept suffering along the way. Becoming the best in the world is uncommon, so athletes need to take uncommon measures to get there. I admire elite athletes so much. Every day, they train hard to reach ambitious goals they've never achieved before. That's no small feat!

Many athletes have shown me that we rarely reach our actual limits, even if our brains are telling us that we have. One such athlete often disregards restrictive thoughts generated by his self-talk. If doubts should arise concerning his ability to take on a new challenge, he stubbornly chooses to put them to the test. He pushes his limits until he can prove whether the doubts were justified or not. Usually, they never are.

> Our minds will quit on us way before our bodies will.

Elite athletes willingly put themselves in situations where they are vulnerable in order to challenge their mental game. They usually get to a point where they're able to dominate these situations and thereafter become more comfortable, and less vulnerable in dealing with them. Anything can happen during competitions, so athletes must be trained to react properly when things don't go as planned.

Practice sessions are also called *training* sessions for a reason. Coaches train athletes to reach their full potential and be as ready as they can be. The objective is always to get better today than you were the day before. Ultimately, becoming an international level athlete is like learning to walk for a baby: it's extremely difficult, but doable.

Sisu-like perseverance is a skill that evolves over time, whether we're learning to ski, use new software, or deal with a demanding boss. At first, it's hard to stay positive. We question why we got into this in the first place. We may question our own abilities. We may even consider giving up. Yet if we persist, the task gradually becomes easier.

Demonstrating *sisu* means being stubborn, especially at the beginning when the challenge seems impossible to overcome. We train our muscles to become stronger physically, so we must train our brains to become stronger mentally so that we can persevere. Strong muscles equal physical endurance; relentless perseverance equals mental endurance.

> We must fall. We must fail. We must make mistakes. Failures tell us what we need to do to evolve.

Every Olympian was a beginner before they became a champion; becoming an Olympian at work is no different.

Chip away

While still a student, I worked in residential construction during the summer to pay the bills. A bricklayer was called in to fabricate a stone wall on the facade of the house. Using a sledgehammer, this specialist had to break bigger stones into smaller pieces that were the size he wanted. Needless to say, it was backbreaking work.

He could strike the stone fifteen times, and it still wouldn't break. Then, after hammering away, it would suddenly break. *Crack!* I learned an important lesson from that man on that day. We should never underestimate the impact of repeated effort.

When we can't see an immediate result, many of us give up, which, in theory, is understandable because the brain likes to be rewarded immediately for its efforts. It requires patience and physical toughness to get to the sixteenth hammer strike! After all, repeated effort is a decisive factor in becoming a true winner.

I told this bricklayer story to Canadian judoka Antoine Valois-Fortier. We were three years out from the 2016 Olympic Games. Looking ahead, Antoine had his eyes on a few tough opponents, especially a Frenchman and a Brazilian, who could potentially block his way to the podium in Rio. The problem was, Antoine had never beaten these two rivals in the past. Was he capable of beating them in the near future? Antoine had his doubts.

So we used the bricklayer metaphor as inspiration. Rather than having a goal of beating them as quickly as possible, we decided it was smarter to focus on simply closing the gap, one bout at a time. Antoine wanted to make sure the fights became tighter and tighter, and hoped that the tide would eventually turn. *Just keep chipping away.* As expected, Antoine suffered a few more losses against these hardened judokas, but the gap was indeed closing.

The sixteenth sledgehammer strike took place at the 2014 World Championships in Chelyabinsk, Russia. And what a strike it was: Antoine beat the Brazilian *and* the Frenchman to capture his first World Championship medal!

Whatever you're currently working on, just keep chipping away.

PHD = *sisu*

Nope, I'm not talking about the doctoral degree, but rather an acronym that stands for three important concepts that a corporate client uses to hone his *sisu*. During our sessions, he often describes the challenges he faces in his company, and I can certainly confirm that the issues are unbelievably complex!

The *P* stands for *patience*, an important element of the *sisu* philosophy. He defines patience as *accepting that things will unfold in a completely different order than originally anticipated*. The key word here is *accepting*, which is easier said than done. This corporate Olympian told me that, without patience, there's no way that he can be in *sisu* mode. In fact, he regrets how patience is a lost virtue in the working world. You probably note its absence, too, every day.

The *H* stands for *humility*. He willingly acknowledges that he doesn't have all the answers to manage the crises at work. He is recognized by his peers as a highly intelligent man. He put his cleverness to work by surrounding himself with a solid team. Coming from a team sport background, he knows that responding to the huge challenges as a group is a lot more efficient than facing them solo.

The D stands for *discipline*. Let me tell you, I've rarely seen such military-like discipline in a corporate leader. He defines discipline as *the ability to still accomplish one task at a time when you really don't feel like doing it*. To feed his fire, he congratulates himself every time he overcomes his reluctance and wins the mental battle. Every battle won only strengthens his *sisu*.

Thanks to this acronym, he stays cool when things get hot and always seems to make the right choices, even though he deals with complicated files.

This guy is so clever, he deserves a PhD right after his name!

Bounce back from failure

Our failures teach us important lessons so that we can get better. If we let ourselves get crushed by them, it becomes nearly impossible to recognize the constructive elements. Therefore, you must learn to reset so you can benefit from the lessons learned. Olympians know all too well what it means to rebound from failure. When you see them celebrating a win on TV, keep in mind that they've been knocked over several times before stepping on a podium.

As an avid sports fan, I watched a lot of the Turin Olympic Games in 2006. I was studying sports psychology at the time and loved drawing parallels between what I was learning and what was happening on television. One athlete that quickly caught my attention was Japanese figure skater Shizuka Arakawa. She had a unique presence, a certain je ne sais quoi that set her apart from the other skaters. However, I might have been biased because I do have a strong appreciation for the Japanese and their culture. They are a proud and hardworking people that never back down from a challenge.

Glued to the television set, I watched Arakawa nail her short program. She was sitting in third place behind an American and a Russian. Again, I noticed a spark in her eyes and some spunk in her persona. I was hooked! I had lots of studying to do, but it didn't matter; I wasn't going to miss her next skate, the long program.

There she was, at center ice, getting into position to kick off her final skate. She knew she had to be perfect. Standing still waiting for the music to commence, she displayed a mix of grace and courage. She looked like a samurai ready for war. Her mind-blowing performance gave her 191.34 points, enough for first place with a staggering eight-point lead over the American skater. That day, Shizuka became the first Japanese woman to win Olympic gold in figure skating.

The next day, a reporter asked her what the key to her success was. With her gentle Japanese manners, Shizuka said confidently, "I earned this gold medal because I found the courage to get up after falling more than twenty thousand times during my career." The sports psychology student in me was awed by that answer. Music to my ears! She embodied the *sisu* principle beautifully.

Are the Japanese and Finns cousins?

Four years after Shizuka Arakawa's triumph, I was working at Cirque du Soleil's headquarters, where I coached a Japanese artist to get him mentally prepared to join a show on a global tour.

After months of training, the time had come for him to join the show. Before heading to the airport, he made sure to thank every one of us who had coached him during his time in Montreal. He dropped by my office to give me a package, carefully wrapped in colorful paper adorned with Japanese symbols. Curious, I unwrapped the gift to discover a papier-mâché doll. I thanked him for the kind gesture, but he noticed my confused expression. Through an interpreter, he explained that this Daruma doll brings luck, prosperity, and perseverance while its owner is trying to reach a desired goal. As I held it in my hands, I noticed that it was round like a Buddha, with no arms, no legs, and no eyes.

In his element, the young Japanese performer mentioned that the owner draws a right eye only once they have set a personal goal. Then, the figurine must be placed somewhere where its owner can see it as a reminder every day. Within sight, within mind, remember?

I pointed out that the doll's base was heavy. Being bottom heavy, the doll can be knocked over, but it will always bounce back to an upright position. "Wanting to bounce back after getting knocked down defines Japanese culture," he said. I took a guess that the left eye could only be drawn once the owner's goal had been achieved. "Very good! I'm not surprised the mental performance coach guessed right!" he said teasingly.

This buddha-like figurine was such a nice gift. After he left, I placed it on my desk and spontaneously made a connection between the doll and the Japanese skater's statement to the reporter. Shizuka may not have been short and round with no eyes, however, just like the Daruma, she did get up thousands of times after falling.

The winding road to success

The route to success is always strewn with obstacles. When a client has an ambitious goal in mind, I put all the cards on the table. *It won't be smooth sailing. There will be highs and lows.* I insist on conveying this message from the get-go because our brains like to anticipate and understand the stakes involved. That way, we have a clear understanding of what we're getting into. Some people prefer not knowing the hefty challenges ahead, but I disagree. To me, going in blind is a recipe for disaster.

As an example, when a talented young athlete dreams of becoming world champion, I lay down the facts.

"So, you think you can become world champion . . . can you see yourself:

- "Being patient as never before?
- "Overcoming the most difficult obstacles in your life?
- "Pushing in training when all you can think about is quitting?
- "Being extremely selfish and obsessed with your sport, even if it means leaving your family and close friends behind?
- "Taking massive risks that could lead to humiliation and several injuries?; or
- "Pushing your physiological boundaries until you throw up?

"And one more thing. All of this may not be enough, because you can't control the external factors that will come into play. You may come in second or fourth or sixth. If you see yourself in all these situations, then, yes, you have a chance of becoming world champion."

The same rules apply to workers who want to climb the echelons of the company and reach the summit.

When the cards are on the table, the process becomes concrete, making it easier to prepare for the hardships ahead and to adjust the details along the way.

The path to success is never a straight line. If we want to climb the ranks or win a championship, we must find a way to persevere regardless of the circumstances. No matter the performance field, I encourage clients to dream big. My job is to make sure they have enough *sisu* to roll with the punches along the way.

> Not running into any obstacles doesn't make you amazing. It only means that your goal wasn't challenging enough.

Failure leads to success

We need to fail to learn from mistakes, but failure also pushes us to take action. Winning over and over again loses its value to a certain extent. Over time, we can become complacent and lose sight of our goal. In sports jargon, we commonly say that an athlete is "hungry" to describe their mood going into a game after losing a few. We are hungry for the win that got away.

I would argue that Tessa Virtue and Scott Moir's gold medal performance in PyeongChang resulted from a failure. Let me explain.

December 2017. We were in Nagoya, Japan, for Grand Prix Finals, only two months before the Games. Tessa and Scott were coming off an impressive winning streak of eleven victories in fourteen months. They ended up skating well, but their performance didn't do justice to their remarkable talents. Their French rivals, on the other hand, skated beautifully and beat Tessa and

Scott for the first time. Tessa and Scott didn't lose this competition; they were beaten by better skaters.

Still, it was painful, like a punch in the gut. But the contrast between winning and losing paved the way for two months of exceptional training. A taste of failure was the wake-up call they needed to realize that they couldn't take anything for granted. It put them on a mission of redemption. So much so that one month after their gruelling loss, Tessa and Scott won the national title with two world record scores, including an unimaginable perfect mark for their free dance. The loss had roused the beast!

During that same time frame, freestyle skier Mikaël Kingsbury was gearing up for the last World Cup event before the PyeongChang Games, held in Mont-Tremblant, Quebec. Like Tessa and Scott, Mikaël had just won a whopping thirteen World Cups in a row. He was on fire! But in Mont-Tremblant, the skiing gods had other plans in mind. His main competitor, Ikuma Horishima, performed magnificently to dethrone the King. This time, Mikaël finished second; Horishima beat him fair and square.

Mik was livid! Despite his disappointment, I was convinced that the loss was the best thing that could have happened to him heading to the Games. He was running the risk of arriving in PyeongChang feeling overconfident and ahead of himself. The bitter taste that remained from Mont-Tremblant was enough to make him focus on the slightest little details of his final preparation. To his credit, he did it better than we could have ever imagined. Mikael would tell you that this rare second-place finish played a decisive role in him becoming Olympic champion.

> You only really know how much you want
> something when you don't have it anymore.

Another contrasting situation struck me, but this time it happened during the Olympic Games. Canadian snowboarder Max Parrot competed in an event called slopestyle, a freestyle contest that takes place on an obstacle course that includes a variety of rails and small jumps to start. The second half of the course holds a series of bigger jumps that can propel the riders as high as forty feet in the air and end up landing more than eighty feet farther down the slope. With its competitors' displays of breathtaking maneuvers, slopestyle has become one of the most popular winter sporting events.

The snowboarders first compete in a qualification event, with only the top twelve advancing to finals. The goal is to ride the course as cleanly as possible, executing creative tricks to impress the judges and accumulate the most points. Inspired and focused, Max qualified in first place. Mission accomplished.

The day before the finals, Max rode beautifully in training, executing his run perfectly not once, but twice. Things were going just as planned, and he felt extremely confident. There's no better feeling going into an Olympic final!

Riders get three goes to complete the course the best they can. In a best-out-of-three format, every run is judged, but only your top score is kept to determine the final ranking. For the finals, the lineup is in reverse order based on the qualification results. Since Max had finished first, he was the last to take the course for every attempt.

On the morning of the finals, Max woke up feeling great. Motivated and energized, he was eager to compete for an Olympic medal. We took the shuttle bus together to the mountain. I sensed that he was a little nervous, but the butterflies were definitely flying in formation. When we arrived, we quickly noticed that the mountain winds had picked up. To stay focused, Max began his warm-up as usual. As the first riders took to the course, it was obvious that they weren't jumping as high as they had wanted to. The weather conditions became a game changer. During his warm-up runs, Max wasn't able to stomp his landings the way he had the day before.

This was the first contrast.

Max began to question everything. "Should I change my run? Should I modify my jumps?" After thinking about it, he kept his run as it was.

During his first attempt, he executed the top part of the course well. The plan for the second of the three bigger jumps was to pull off a triple, or three back flips. First flip, yes! Second flip, yes! Third flip . . . bang! Max crashed from roughly fifty feet in the air. From my vantage point at the bottom of the course, I saw his head hit the ground hard. I held my breath. Finally, he made his way to the bottom of the course. With a bloody chin, he was clearly stunned from what just happened. His frustration was palpable. Worried for his safety, I asked him if he was going to simplify his second jump to make it easier to land. "No," he said. "I need to try it again to find out if I can pull it off despite this wind. Otherwise, I may regret it."

We looked each other in the eye. We bumped fists as we usually did, and he headed off to the chairlift.

He started the second run brilliantly. He executed the first half of the course even better than he had on his first attempt. The first of the three bigger jumps was perfect. Then came the second jump where Max fell hard the first time. In the in-run to the jump, he gathered as much speed as possible, hoping that he would get more height this time. He kicked into the air . . . and fell heavily on his neck again!

He was fuming with frustration and anger, so I gave him some time to cool off before talking to him. The stakes were high. Only one run remained to get him on the podium. Finally, he asked me, "What should I be thinking up there before my last run?" He knew the answer to that question. He'd been in similar situations before. Experienced as he was, the required mental tools to manage this moment were in his back pocket. So, I threw the question right back at him: "What do *you* think you should be thinking about?"

I've learned over the years that, under these kinds of circumstances, it's so much more powerful if the athlete takes responsibility for the moment and comes up with their own answers. I wanted him to be in control. As if thinking out loud, he mumbled, "I must change the jump. There's too much wind (*adapt to change*). I'm handling the rails quite well. At least that part's going my way (*feed the fire with small victories*). I'm going to focus on my breathing on the way up — that'll help me calm down (*find the Olympian calm*). I'm going to think about little Max, aged nine, who has fun in the snow park (*connecting with his* why)." We went through our little routine again and . . . presto! Next thing I knew, he was back on the chairlift for his final run.

It felt like an eternity passed before his turn came. Finally, I saw him on the big screen, where he appeared to be in control. Max was the last competitor to go. If he nailed this run, the snowboarding community knew he would rank among the top finishers. Still, his performance had to be flawless. There was some work to be done.

Max was about to take off, ready to tackle the course one last time. I knew he had what it took to get it done, but I was still extremely nervous. He got through the first half with no problem whatsoever. It looked easy. So far, so good. He successfully landed the first big jump and was approaching the second jump. Everyone was holding their breath, especially the event leaders. Max simplified his maneuver just a tad and went for the double instead of the triple, and he stomped it! The crowd was fired up. One more jump to go, Max seemed in full control of the situation. He hit the jump, first flip, second flip, third flip . . . he did it!

I burst with joy along with the spectators gathered at the bottom of the course. What an accomplishment under such enormous pressure! The judges took their time. Another eternity seemed to pass. Then, 86 flashed on the big screen. Max had won silver, his first Olympic medal. I couldn't hold it in any longer, laughing and crying at the same time. What a moment! We were all so proud of Max.

I can draw several lessons from Max's slopestyle experience in PyeongChang. Among them, the most important one is arguably the fact that he never perceived the two falls as failures. Despite his justifiable frustration, the falls became evidence, a body of necessary information he gathered to adjust and successfully master the third and final attempt. He remained realistic and intelligent throughout the process. He also never gave up despite the bloody chin, the sore neck, or the annoyance of falling twice. He demonstrated *sisu* on snow.

Ten months later, Max found out he had to battle for his life. He was diagnosed with Hodgkin's lymphoma, the same type of cancer that hockey legend Mario Lemieux had back in the 1990s. Max immediately underwent a series of twelve chemotherapy treatments. He announced the horrible news to the world during a press conference. As I sat beside Max, a reporter asked me about his mental state. "Snowboarding is a dangerous sport," I said. "Max puts his life on the line every day. He knows how to deal with fear, and he is as stubborn as hell! When he wants something, he usually gets it. Max always demonstrated unbelievable perseverance when challenged. It won't be any different this time. He will beat the cancer."

And Max did just that.

I was honoured to travel with Max for his return to competition. On August 31, 2019, after an eight-month absence, and only two months since his last chemo treatment, Max won gold at the X Games in Norway. He also won his next two competitions, including gold at the X Games in Aspen. Max is the epitome of *sisu*.

The bamboo tree, Olympian of the forest

Sisu requires adapting to unexpected change, as we've just seen. In moments of turbulence, it enables us to remain calm and stay the course towards the ultimate goal. I remember witnessing an impressive tropical storm while traveling through Southeast Asia. There was a bamboo forest next door to the place I was staying at. During the storm, the small bamboo stalks swayed wildly in all directions, whipped by the violent winds. They bent over so far that I expected them to snap. When I woke up the next morning, none of them had. The trees were as straight as an arrow. The intertwined strands that make up this tree allow it to withstand the worst storms.

Bamboo trees adapt just as well to wet as they do to sandy soils, and to hot temperatures as well as they do to cooler ones. Bamboo is also one of the fastest-growing trees on earth. Why? Because it doesn't need ideal conditions to grow; it simply adapts.

We would be able to embody *sisu* better if our brains were to react like bamboo trees, with their ability to adapt and endure. What happens to you in moments of intense stress?

- Do you tend to bend or crack?
- Do you need perfect conditions to perform well, or are you able to adapt regardless of the conditions?
- Can your colleagues count on you when the going gets tough?

> You don't need to be in exceptional shape to deliver an exceptional performance. It's also possible to be excellent in difficult conditions.

The unflappable poker player

A few years ago, I met a professional poker player who told me that having an agile mind in his profession is imperative, otherwise, he would get eaten alive. These card players have to know themselves well so that they can deal with their emotions at all times. Consequently, he relied extensively on mental training. "I must remind myself that I have no control over the cards I'm dealt. So there's no reason to overreact. I just have to be ready for any eventuality, then show my poker face."

The same rule applies at work. For the most part, we don't control the projects we're given, so we must be ready for any eventuality. This card player relied immensely on self-control. "Our brains are wired to adequately respond to situations, whatever they may be. We just have to be ready for them. The moment when I first see the cards is critical. When I look at them, I *choose* to remain calm and unperturbed. If I'm reactive or impulsive, my opponents will notice, and that's giving them an advantage."

To increase the drama of televised poker, the players are sometimes outfitted with heart monitors to show the viewers the physiological variations that poker players experience during a game. As things heat up, the best players maintain a composed appearance even though their heart is racing, hence the term *poker face*.

Elite poker players don't wait to draw a good hand to make a move. They find ways to win regardless of how good the cards are. If their hand is horrible, the players can always *bluff*.

> If you wait for perfect conditions,
> you'll never get things done.

Poker faces are also practical at work. We can't choose our cards, but we can choose how to play them.

Remaining cold-blooded is a key part of *sisu*.

Strengthen your *sisu*

Clearly, we can't master the *sisu* philosophy from one day to the next. It takes hard work. Below are a few tips and strategies to strengthen your inner *sisu*.

GPS "sensalization"

The main reason people are unable to tap into their *sisu* is their inability to adequately respond to adversity. When a problem is too hot to handle, they freeze and panic. Their brains aren't able to shift into solution mode. Here are a few questions to ask yourself before undertaking the strategy suggested below:

- Will you encounter some kind of adversity in the year ahead? *We can certainly assume so.*
- In the coming month? *Without a doubt.*
- In the coming week? *In all likelihood.*
- Today? *Possibly.*

Whether we like it or not, adversity is always just around the corner. A life without any bumps on the road doesn't exist. As a result, we must expect adversity and be ready for it. Most events that will throw you off in the future are usually events that challenged you in the past. This means that, for the most part, you should be able to see them coming and prepare accordingly.

Like most drivers, you've used a GPS at some point to get to a destination as quickly as possible. You enter the address and the itinerary magically appears on-screen. There's even a voice to guide you along the way. Some days, the route is less than ideal due to construction, detours, accidents, or general road repairs. But it's okay because this gadget is programmed to see what road obstacles lie ahead.

Does the GPS complain when a roadblock suddenly appears? Does it get mad about later arrival times? Of course not! Your road assistant calmly *recalculates the route* to indicate the road to take, while we can hardly contain ourselves.

Humans don't often function like machines, although it may be better to act like one when facing a threatening obstacle. Great athletes work hard to make their brains operate like a GPS: when facing an obstacle, they can remain calm, reassess, and quickly come up with a solution. Occasionally, they also get flustered because their brains are not in the proper mental state to think straight. It's the limbic system that kicks in and leads to dramatization, bad decision-making, and impulsive and undesired behavior.

To counter this, I created a mental training exercise called *GPS sensalization*, which resembles fire drills at school. We ask kids to rehearse a specific protocol, which typically includes a step-by-step process to safely leave the building. These rehearsals create a neurological pathway in children's minds so that they know exactly what to do when the fire alarm goes off and, more importantly, to avoid panic.

> Because we can anticipate most future stressful moments, GPS sensalization can help to program a desired response.

In this exercise, there are three columns to be filled. In the first column, you describe the stressful situation. In the second, you list the symptoms (physical and mental) resulting from the stressful situation. In the third, you write the solution you believe is ideal. Let's go through the exercise using two examples: a figure skater and a worker.

FIGURE SKATER		
Stressful Situation	Symptoms (mental and physical)	Desired Responses
Dead-tired legs with thirty seconds to go	• heavy legs • changing posture • excessive sweating • negative self-talk: "Uh-oh! I hate this feeling."	• fix my posture • remind myself that it's normal to feel pain and to sweat excessively • be in the moment by telling myself to "feel the ice" and "focus on the next sequence"

WORKER		
Stressful Situation	Symptoms (mental and physical)	Desired Responses
Presenting in front of colleagues, managers, executives	• speaking too quickly • sweaty palms • fixed stare • negative self-talk: "My colleagues don't like my presentation."	• speak slower • think about breathing calmly • look people in the eye • smile from time to time

Once you've filled out the three columns, the next step is to run through each case in your mind. Through sensalization, imagine and feel yourself facing the stressful situation you wrote in the first column, then let yourself experience the unpleasant symptoms in the second column, and finally, shift to executing the desired responses in the third. To ensure efficiency, running the scenario for thirty to sixty seconds every day is enough to program the neurological route in your brain to respond efficiently at the appropriate time.

The most common mistake I see in regard to visualization is that most people mainly use it to picture a flawless performance, as if they relied on columns one and three only. You know what I mean; that time you closed your eyes and imagined your presentation going so well, you received a standing ovation. We know that, realistically, things rarely happen this way. If, during this same presentation, you were asked an embarrassing question, you might have struggled to be quick on your feet. The neural pathway wasn't created. GPS system error!

I teach GPS sensalization to basically every client who prepares for important events that will generate stressful moments. If you feel there are several stressors to prepare for, that's perfectly fine. Better prepared means more confidence heading into the event.

Figure skaters Tessa Virtue and Scott Moir trained their internal GPS in preparation for PyeongChang, just like boxer Marie-Ève Dicaire relied heavily on neurological programming to be crowned world champion. This same technique has helped individuals master job interviews and surgeons perform intricate surgery.

Training your internal GPS helps you tap into *sisu*.

Rely on consistency

In today's world, we are expected to be at the top of our game on a daily basis. But is it realistic to think that we can always perform at our best? Beware of unrealistic expectations, especially when we're the ones setting them. I mean, would it be fair to ask a golfer to birdie every hole? Or expect a baseball player to slug a home run every time he stepped up to the plate? Well, the same goes for meetings, project assignments, and interactions with colleagues, customers, and suppliers.

When clients wish to always deliver better performances, I encourage them instead to focus on having a *consistent mindset*. I suggest this because we control our way of seeing things, but we can't control external factors that impact our performances.

Let's go back to the manager who delivered a presentation. He won't have any control whatsoever over technical problems that may arise. His presentation would suffer for it, but would he be a failure due to a technical problem for which he's not responsible? Not at all.

My friends who work with Major League Baseball players were telling me that the best hitters rely heavily on specific pre-at-bat routines. Whether it's a regular season or a playoff game, their mental approach is the same. This consistency fosters a positive psychological framework and normalizes pressure moments, increasing the likelihood of success.

Obviously, a consistent, constructive mindset doesn't *guarantee* success, but it does increase its likelihood.

During coaching sessions, I tell Olympians all the time to stop focusing on the gold medal. Instead, I suggest concentrating on the execution of the elements related to their performance and then see what comes out of it. It's a subtle difference that can have a major impact. The focus is more on the process, rather than the result, which makes it easier for the athlete to persevere.

The lesson to be learned: a consistent mentality fosters a consistent performance.

Why am I doing this again?

From time to time, it's beneficial to remind ourselves what drove us to practice our profession in the first place. For what reasons did we choose our line of work? This is also true for a personal challenge, like getting into shape or learning another language.

It's a simple mental training technique that helps you persist during hard times or when you feel you're about to quit. Below are a few examples:

- When a gymnast doesn't feel like lifting weights, he recalls that becoming an Olympic champion was his childhood dream.
- When there's no motivation to diet and exercise, remember that you're doing it to shed those extra pounds to feel fit and healthy again.

- When the exhausted teacher is thinking about quitting her job, she thinks about her positive impact on students' lives.
- When the manager can no longer motivate her employees, she remembers that she always dreamed of leading a corporate team.

Bringing additional awareness to the fundamental reasons distances you from the difficulty at that moment in time and helps put things into perspective. It's that little kick in the pants that we sometimes need!

A few years ago, I helped a medical student get ready for her plastic surgery exams. The passing grade was 70 percent. If you failed, you had to wait a full year before taking them again. She had already attempted the exams twice. Her self-confidence level was low, to say the least. We spoke a lot about the *sisu* philosophy. I explained that for the Finns, the real victory was never, ever giving up. To fill up her emotional tank, I also encouraged her to think back to her reasons for wanting to become a surgeon in the first place.

These tips struck the right chords. She reconnected with the motivators that lay in her gut. Suddenly, she had a *sisu*-like determination to do everything she could to pass. A few months later, she crushed the exam on her third attempt! Today, she's an excellent surgeon and living her dream!

Look back, too!

In 2011, I scratched off an item on my bucket list. I cycled from Berlin, Germany, to Dubrovnik, Croatia: 1,500 miles in fifty-two days carrying 50 pounds of gear. Needless to say, this cycling trip challenged me more than once. I remember one day when I pedalled into a head wind for eighty miles. That day never seemed to end!

At the time, it was the most challenging bike touring trip of my life. To optimize my preparation, I spoke to a tour guide who knew the European bike routes very well. He shared advice that paid dividends.

"When cycling, we always look ahead. We forget that we're only seeing half the landscape! Behind us is another reality, a completely different perspective." The wise man continued, "This trip won't be easy. There will be moments when you'll be dead tired. Your brain will start thinking about the distance left to ride, and you'll want to quit. When this moment comes, stop, get off your bike, and look back. The satisfaction you'll get from seeing how far you've already come will give you extra energy to continue."

His advice was on point. This one day in the Czech Republic, I rode approximately twenty mid-size climbs over fifty miles, and then had about ten more to go before reaching my destination. I was exhausted! I heard the man's voice telling me to stop, get off my bike, and look back. I did. The landscape was s-p-e-c-t-a-c-u-l-a-r! The golden sun was setting over fields of bright-yellow rapeseeds that stretched as far as the eye could see. No cars and no people in sight. Only the bare, winding hills that I rode. Magically, the last ten miles suddenly weren't as intimidating.

Whatever our occupation, we spend a considerable amount of time looking ahead. The meeting this afternoon, the assignment due tomorrow, the presentation next week, or the numbers to hit in six months. When the workload is heavy, paying too much attention to what's left can lead to discouragement. Sometimes, we just need to STOP:

Stop
Turn
Observe
(become aware of) Progress

Use it. You'll notice that it boosts motivation and counteracts the desire to quit.

Right now, take a moment to enjoy the progress you've made. Look at the road traveled since last week or last month.

This exercise is also useful for groups. Why not start a meeting by sharing the progress made on a project at work?

The first steps are the hardest

So many people quit before they've even started. Take jogging, for example. Once you get going, you're rolling! It's before we walk out the door that we struggle. We have to coax ourselves to overcome the excuses. *It's cold. It's rainy. I'm tired.* When we finally get over that hump, our bodies start moving, we pick up the pace, and we're out the door. Our brains are naturally lazy, so this kind of behavior is absolutely normal.

> A brain works like a rocket. Lots of energy is needed to take off, but once it's launched, nothing can stop it.

Rolling a heavy rock is another metaphor. You must generate lots of power to move it, but once it starts to roll, it requires minimal force to guide it in the right direction. I call this "the mental inertia principle."

What tasks require stamina at the start?

- Answering a bunch of emails?
- Working on an exhaustive report?
- Preparing a meeting?
- Filing paperwork?

Keep in mind that the early struggles are temporary. Like the rocket, once your brain gets going, just steer it in the right direction. Three, two, one, blast off!

Dare to be unconventional

Despite all the strategies that I've shared to sharpen your *sisu*, every so often we just run out of answers. That's when we need to become creative and start thinking outside the box.

I would like to end this chapter with a tribute to the *sisu* philosophy through an unconventional story that I share during my talks. The main character is one of the best leaders I know. He's a big reason why I got into mental performance coaching. As a baseball coach, he's not afraid to opt for unusual measures for the good of the team. His name is André Lachance.

In my early twenties, I got to join the support staff of Canada's women's national baseball team. It was my first time working with an elite sports organization. As is often the case with first experiences, I will never forget it.

Let's turn back the clocks to 2004. The national team was competing in two international tournaments: a World Series in Uozu, Japan, and a World Cup in Edmonton, Canada. Our performance in Japan was not one for the history books. We ended the tournament with two crushing losses. The twelve-hour plane ride back to Western Canada was pretty quiet. Everyone was disgusted with the turn of events, especially Coach Lachance.

But we had to turn the page. The World Cup in Edmonton was quickly approaching. To gear up for the tournament, we organized a series of exhibition games against midget-level boys' teams in Alberta.

What a mistake!

The boys' level of play was far superior to that of our women. To our surprise, the boys clobbered us four games to none. We also got cranked during our first game of the tournament against Japan, for a total of seven losses in a row. The team's confidence hit a record low after no wins in three weeks of play. A few days later, we would be playing the powerful Americans. At this point, no one was taking the Canadians seriously.

The evening before our practice to prepare to face the Americans, we coaches met in André's hotel room to discuss which drills to prioritize. Each of us suggested something, but not Coach Lachance, who said nothing. We could practically hear the gears turning in his brain! Finally, he spoke up. "We know how to play defensively. We know how to hit the ball. But what we *don't* *know* is how to win! We want to play like we practice, right? So, tomorrow, we're going to practice to win!" We looked at each other without really understanding what he meant.

The next morning, the players huddled to receive practice instructions. André explained that the first hour would be allocated to defensive and batting drills, and the last thirty minutes were to be a surprise.

An hour later, André gathered the team together. "We haven't won in three weeks. Experiencing the sweet taste of victory would be awesome, wouldn't you say?" Everyone nodded. At that very moment, the Americans walked into the stands. Their practice was scheduled after ours.

André gave his instructions. "You're all going to line up, single file, behind home plate in the order of your sweater numbers. Grab a helmet and a bat. Here's what we're going to do. We are simulating a game, Canada versus USA. We're going to pretend that we are in the last inning. The score is tied 2-2. There are two outs and we have a runner on third base. Each of you will go up to bat, one at a time. A coach will stand on the mound and pretend to throw a fastball, down the middle. You will pretend to hit a base hit, over second base, to right-center field. You will sprint to first base and celebrate as if you had driven in your fictitious teammate for real. Be creative! We three coaches will stand near first base to mark your acting abilities out of ten. We'll see who deserves the best mark. Ready? Go!"

Imagine the players' faces when they understood how ridiculous the whole thing was. And with the Americans and many reporters sitting in the stands to enjoy the show!

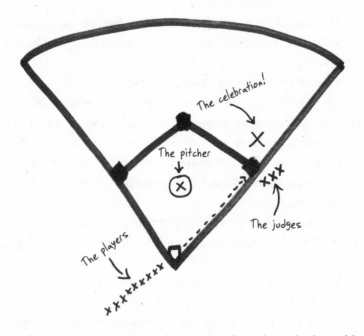

The players took their places. The first player had trouble breaking the ice. Her embarrassed behavior earned a unanimous 2 out of 10. However, the following celebrations improved little by little. The exercise was working. The fifth player had really cooked up an Oscar-worthy performance. She walked up to the plate, signalled to the pitcher to *bring it on*. She spat (baseball players do it, not sure why), scratched some dirt in the batters' box, swung, and took off running to first base as if her life depended on it. She took off her jersey (she was wearing an undershirt), whipped it around over her head like a cowboy lasso, yelled "Yee-haaa!" and mimicked the gestures of a cowboy roping the legs of a steer in a rodeo show.

Each of us gave her a 10!

Everyone was laughing so hard their ribs ached! The team played along so well. With one player left to go, André asked the entire team to join her at first base to simulate a win by the entire team. A brilliant way to finish!

It only took thirty minutes to forget seven losses.

The next day, there was no more pretending. Several thousand Canadian fans gathered in the stands to witness the great Canada-USA rivalry.

True story: In the last inning, the score was tied 1-1, with a girl on second. The atmosphere was electric. It was a chance to beat the Americans on home soil and make history. This was a pressure moment, and everyone on the team demonstrated their Olympian calm. I was sitting in the players' dugout when one of the women stood up and said, "We rehearsed this yesterday. We're going to win!"

Our player hit a liner in the gap in right-center field. The player on second had the time to round third base and force the play at home.

We did it! The Canadians beat the Americans 2-1!

The team was ecstatic. A historic victory, performed in our own backyard. The next day, one of the local newspapers wrote, "Canada Practised to Win and it Worked!"

The players stressed that the simulation drill was a game changer. They never once doubted that winning was possible. Practicing to win was exactly what the team needed in those circumstances. This wonderful display of *sisu* led to our first podium finish, a bronze medal against the tough Australians.

When adversity strikes and you're scrambling for answers, consider taking drastic measures by thinking outside the box. Coach Lachance's philosophy is, "If you think like everyone, you'll be like everyone." The Canadian team was desperate and needed an alternative solution to succeed.

It takes unconventional measures to get unconventional results, in baseball as at work.

CONCLUSION

On your mark. Get set. Go!

Our adventure together is drawing to a close, but the process of you becoming an Olympian at work has just begun!

Thank you for taking the time to read this sharing of knowledge. I hope that the content and anecdotes, which have marked my career over the years, enlightened you and sometimes made you smile.

It has been an honor to accompany you on this journey, and I thank you for this.

You've certainly noticed how much I love my work. I still need to pinch myself from time to time as I realize what a great privilege it is for me to convey my passion, whether through my talks, my coaching, or this book.

For my part, I feel like I've gone through my own Olympic Games . . . on paper! Accessing, unravelling, and organizing my knowledge so I could share it with you was not an easy feat.

Now that we've come to the end, I can say that every second of every minute dedicated to this book was well worth it. When I struggled to make sense of my ideas and became irritated because of it, I went back to what mattered the most: doing it for you. Each time, I felt a burst of adrenaline pushing me towards the finish line. I hope that you retained a few nuggets, and more importantly, that I was able to meet a need.

I encourage you to refer back to this book when you feel the need to, whether to reread it or simply flip through it. *Train (Your Brain) Like an Olympian* is not a step-by-step recipe for success. Quite the opposite — I would be pleased if all you took away from it was just one thing.

All of us are expected to perform every day, with the demands at work never ceasing to grow. And our modern society is changing around us at an unbridled pace. Thanks to technology, we are constantly distracted in a world where everything seems to be moving at the speed of light. As a result, we have never been as overwhelmed, tired, or stressed. We need to acknowledge it and prioritize our mental health. Without good health, we don't have much.

Mental preparation can be a compass to guide us through these troubled waters. Even though most of the content is inspired by elite athletes, these tips are for everyone and can offer important benefits for your general well-being.

Mental training also requires constant effort. Fortunately, your brain is wired to naturally grow and progress. Don't limit your mind. Keep feeding it and make sure to challenge it from time to time.

That is exactly what sports champions of all stripes do incredibly well. Throughout my career, I've been blown away by their eagerness to excel. It's such a privilege to work with individuals who strive to reach their full potential. Little do they know just how much they offer me in return.

So, I hope their stories will better equip your brain, your engine that drives performance. As mentioned in the introduction, the goal is not to make you the best in the world in your field, but to offer you ways to improve, period.

In closing, I would like to leave you with something to think about, just as I do during my coaching sessions and talks.

Do your colleagues, friends, and family members have access to the best version of you? If you could improve just one thing, what would it be?

- Adopt a better attitude?
- Improve your concentration?
- Increase your tolerance of pressure and stress?
- Build your self-confidence?
- Demonstrate more *sisu*?

In the end, *Train (Your Brain) Like an Olympian* remains a compilation of knowledge related to mental training. It's what you'll do with it that gives the book its true meaning.

The time has come to discover your inner Olympian.

If you have any questions or comments that you would like to send me, you can do so through this website: www.kambioperformance.com.

On your mark. Get set. Go!

Yours sincerely,

Jean François Ménard is an internationally acclaimed mental performance expert who coaches high achievers in all walks of life. He is the founder of Kambio Performance, a company specializing in mental training and leadership coaching. His clients are proven winners: Olympic gold medalists, Cirque du Soleil artists, Super Bowl and X Games champions, surgeons, musicians, and corporate leaders. He is a bestselling author, a radio personality, and an accomplished speaker who travels the globe to share his knowledge with top-performing companies.

Marie Malchelosse has more than twenty years of experience as a sports journalist. She has covered numerous Olympic games and other major sporting events. Her understanding of elite sport was instrumental in the writing of *Train (Your Brain) Like an Olympian*.